THE LIFE BOOK OF CHRISTMAS • VOLUME TWO

THE
PAGEANTRY
OF
CHRISTMAS

OTHER BOOKS BY THE EDITORS OF LIFE

THE LIFE BOOK OF CHRISTMAS · VOLUME TWO

THE PAGEANTRY OF CHRISTMAS

OTHER BOOKS BY THE EDITORS OF LIFE

THE PAGEANTRY OF CHRISTMAS

BY THE EDITORS OF
LIFE

A
STONEHENGE
BOOK

TIME INCORPORATED, NEW YORK

TIME INC. BOOK DIVISION

Editor Norman P. Ross

Copy Director William Jay Gold   *Art Director* Edward A. Hamilton

Chief of Research Beatrice T. Dobie

Editorial staff for Volume Two of
THE LIFE BOOK OF CHRISTMAS

Editor Stanley Fillmore

Designers Kenneth Hine, Norman Snyder

Text Gerald Simons (Chief), John Stanton, Barbara Elias

Chief Researcher Carlotta Kerwin

Researchers Audrey Foote, Mary Ellen Murphy,
Kaye Neil, Donald Nelson, Jenifer Ratliff, Jean Sulzberger

Picture Researchers Margaret K. Goldsmith, Barbara Sullivan

Art Associate Robert L. Young

Art Assistants James D. Smith, John Newcomb,
Robert McElrath, David Wyland

Copy Staff Marian Gordon Goldman, Rosalind Stubenberg,
Dolores A. Littles

Publisher Jerome S. Hardy

General Manager John A. Watters

LIFE MAGAZINE

Editor Edward K. Thompson

Managing Editor George P. Hunt

Publisher C. D. Jackson

The following individuals and departments of Time
Inc. helped in producing this book: Doris O'Neil, Chief
of the LIFE Picture Library; Content Peckham, Chief
of the Time Inc. Bureau of Editorial Reference; Donald
Bermingham and Clara Applegate of the TIME-LIFE
News Service; Correspondents Gerda Endler (Bonn),
Katharine Sachs (London), Piero Saporiti (Madrid),
Page d'Aulnay and Joseph Harriss (Paris), Gertraud
Lessing (Vienna).

CONTENTS
VOLUME TWO

INTRODUCTION

A distinguished American scholar, Dr. Earl Count, has defined Christmas in these words: it is "a spontaneous drama of the common folk, a prayer, a hymn. All the while that Raphael was painting the Sistine Madonna, Frenchmen building the cathedral of Chartres, English bishops composing the Book of Common Prayer, Handel his *Messiah,* Bach his *B-Minor Mass,* the common people, out of whom these geniuses sprang, were composing Christmas."

They composed it slowly, taking years—even centuries—to complete the task. St. Nicholas, for example, was a bishop in Asia Minor in the Fourth Century. In the Middle Ages, a towering folk legend evolved which credited him with saving sailors in distress *(opposite)* and providing dowries for marriageable maidens. It was not until the 17th Century, when the Dutch who settled New Amsterdam corrupted his name (Saint Nicholas to Sint Klaes to Santa Claus), that he grew into his present role.

The people composed Christmas as an expression of religious devotion and secular pageantry. It is a work that has never ended; it proceeds as vigorously today as it did 1,000 years ago. The story of the people's creation of Christmas is the story of this book, Volume Two in the three-volume LIFE BOOK OF CHRISTMAS.

Volume One re-creates in text and fine art the ageless glory of the first Christmas. In dealing with the development of Christmas pageantry, each chapter of the present volume begins with a quotation that sets the tone of what follows. Each chapter then describes and illustrates a particular period of history, with emphasis on its special contributions to the stream of traditions. Thus Chapter I traces the beginnings of pageantry in the pagan past. It shows how the early Church Fathers, recognizing the superstitious and emotional attachment of the people to their pagan rites, sought to give them a Christian significance. Then follows an anthology of prose, poetry and music, in which the living voices of the era can be heard. The final chapter in the volume offers photographic evidence that the synthesis of Christmas continues still.

Altogether, this volume presents the evolving nature of Christmas, its unfolding and enrichment over the centuries. The world's great art museums and private libraries were searched for glimpses of many different kinds of Christmas: those of real people and legendary figures, of Charlemagne and King Arthur, St. Francis and Shakespeare, Martin Luther and Queen Victoria. All have become part of Christmas. So has the inventive 19th Century New York cartoonist, Thomas Nast, who first sketched the familiar Santa Claus of today.

Here are 20 centuries of glittering Christmas pageantry: parties, pagan rites, knightly tournaments, miracle plays, Lords of Misrule, Boy Bishops, boars' heads, peacock pies, plum puddings, Christmas carols, cards and trees. "The lifeblood of a people is its traditions," Dr. Count says. This book presents the traditions and the lustrous pageantry of Christmas.

—THE EDITORS OF LIFE

I

THE EARLIEST YEARS

I HAVE, UPON MATURE DELIB-eration on the affair of the English, determined upon, viz., that the temples of the idols in that nation ought not to be destroyed; but let the idols that are in them be destroyed; let holy water be made and sprinkled in the said temples, let altars be erected, and relics placed. For if those temples are well built, it is requisite that they be converted from the worship of devils to the service of the true God; that the nation, seeing that their temples are not destroyed, may remove error from their hearts, and knowing and adoring the true God, may the more familiarly resort to the places to which they have been accustomed. . . . For there is no doubt that it is impossible to efface every thing at once from their obdurate minds; because he who endeavours to ascend to the highest place, rises by degrees or steps, and not by leaps.

POPE GREGORY'S LETTER TO AN ENGLISH MISSIONARY

THE MADONNA OF MERCY *dominates this painting in the first church dedicated to Mary, Santa Maria in Trastevere, Rome.*

TURNING
PAGAN RITES
TO THE
PRAISE OF GOD

A SECTION OF MARBLE SLAB *used to shut tombs is marked with the Greek letters "chi" and "rho," identifying the figure as Christ.*

"HOW WONDERFULLY acted Divine Providence that on the day that the Sun was born—Christ should be born." So said St. Cyprian, a Third Century Bishop of Carthage. He was referring to December 25, when the winter days begin to lengthen.

St. Cyprian was ahead of many early Christians. Until 350 A.D., when Pope Julius I proclaimed December 25 as the date of the Nativity, almost every month in the year had, at one time or another, been named by reputable scholars as the likely date of Christ's birth. There is still disagreement about the actual historical date, but for practical purposes Pope Julius' choice has long been accepted by all the churches except the Armenian, which still observes Christmas on January 6.

By the time of Pope Julius' proclamation, Christianity was on its way to becoming a world religion. Its establishment had taken more than 300 years. Eleven Apostles had set out to spread the teachings of their crucified Lord. They had traveled far—St. Peter to Rome; St. Thomas, tradition says, to India. A great organizer, St. Paul, knit the scattered Christian communities into a cohesive and flourishing church.

They and their converts had met sporadic, but always brutal, persecution from the Roman authorities. In 64 A.D. Peter and Paul had been killed when Nero made Christians the scapegoats for his burning of Rome. Worse waves of persecution had followed. In 303 A.D., Emperor Diocletian celebrated the Nativity by putting 20,000 Roman Christians to death by fire. Once again the faithful were driven into their underground tombs, the catacombs *(opposite)*.

But in 313, Emperor Constantine, himself a Christian convert, issued his Edict of Toleration, which legalized Christianity throughout the Roman Empire. And in 392 Theodosius I was to outlaw paganism. It was on this rising tide that Pope Julius declared December 25 the feast of the Nativity.

Christians, for whom Christ was the new beginning and the new light of the world, celebrated His birth in a seasonal tradition which crosscut a number of cultures. During the winter solstice, ancient Mesopotamians performed rites to aid their god Marduk in his struggle against the forces of chaos. At that season, the Greek Zeus began anew his battle against Kronos (Time) and the Titans. The followers of Mithras, a Persian sun-god whose cult was brought to Rome by returning legionaries and became the chief rival of Christianity, celebrated December 25 as *Dies Solis Invicti Nati* (Birthday of the Unconquered Sun). The Romans themselves had long celebrated the solstice season as the Saturnalia, honoring Saturn, the god of agriculture.

During Saturnalia, normal life turned upside down. Gambling was declared legal, courts were closed, and no one could be convicted of a crime. Slaves dressed in their masters' clothes and were served by their masters. A mock king was chosen to rule the festivities: He would turn up at Christmas again, centuries later, as the Lord of Misrule. Lavish holiday banquets featured such delicacies as peacock eggs in pepper sauce. The exchange of gifts became an important part of the festivities. They were simple at first—wax candles or clay dolls—but they slowly grew more elaborate.

Christians began absorbing these old customs and infusing them with Christian meaning in order to help spread the faith. Many Church fathers considered the method dangerous. St. Augustine, the greatest theologian of the Fourth Century, warned his people: "We hold this day holy, not like the pagans because of the birth of the sun, but because of Him who made it."

But most of the Christian missionaries who moved into Central and Western Europe as the Roman Empire crumbled, followed the advice of Gregory the Great. He wrote, in 597, that they should not try to put down pagan customs "upon the sudden," but adapt them "to the praise of God."

In the North, at the Christmas season, the missionaries found the pagan adherents of the gods Woden and Thor battling the winter's evil darkness with huge bonfires. In Central Europe, they found the belief that at the death of the old sun, witches and fiery demons came to earth to destroy the fertility of the new year, and could be dissuaded by presents. In Britain, they found Druids paying tribute to the victory of evergreens over winter's darkness.

The missionaries, heeding Gregory the Great's advice, made no effort to "cut off" the "evil customs." As a result, many of them survive as cherished Christmas traditions of today.

AN EARLY CHRISTIAN MOSAIC, *possibly the earliest known, decorates the ceilings and walls of a catacomb beneath St. Peter's Cathedral, near where St. Peter is said to be buried. The figure represents Christ but the symbol was previously used to portray a pagan sun-god. Such blendings of Hellenistic and Christian thought were common in the first years of the Christian Era.*

FROM UNDERGROUND TOMBS, A RENEWED FAITH

Of all the places where early Christians worshiped, none evokes a grimmer image than the catacombs. These enormous caverns, in some places five stories high, were built between the First and Fifth Centuries as cemeteries, located, by law, outside the city. When persecutions under the Roman emperors intensified, the Christians used the catacombs as places of refuge and prayer.

Paintings on the catacomb walls *(above and opposite)* indicate that the caverns had become real places of worship. Special services were held on the anniversary of a martyr's death, and special burial areas were set aside to the honor of various saints and martyrs.

The tombs made almost perfect refuges from persecution. Elaborate hiding places with secret openings

FOUR MAGI *bear gifts to Virgin and Child in this Fourth Century fresco from the Catacombs of Domitilla, Rome. The number of Wise Men varied in art works until the Sixth Century, when three became accepted.*

into adjoining quarries, blocked areas and false exits abounded. It has been estimated that more than 500 miles of galleries existed in the catacombs of Rome. Smaller ones harbored refugees in Sicily, Tuscany, Africa, Egypt and Asia Minor. One of the enduring legends of the Roman catacombs is that St. Peter preached in them and that he is buried in their endless labyrinth.

A CHRISTIAN WOMAN *lifts her arms in prayer in a Third Century fresco from the Roman Catacombs of Domitilla. In early Christian art, this figure, called an "orant," was used as a symbol of the faithful dead.*

13

THE BIRTH OF ST. NICHOLAS, *his call to God's serv-*
ice and his gifts to the three poor maidens are depicted
(left to right) in this panel painted by Fra Angelico.

ST. NICHOLAS OF BARI *saves a ship and greets an en-*
voy (right). The Fra Angelico panels on these pages
were painted for San Domenico Church, Perugia.

THE SERENITY OF ST. LUCY *stands out in this detail from a mosaic*
illustrating a procession of virgin martyrs at Ravenna, Italy. Devo-
tion to the devout and saintly girl goes back to the Fourth Century.

SAINTS TO HONOR IN THE DAYS TO COME

Two of the early Christian saints are especially honored during the Christmas season—St. Nicholas on December 6 in Holland and St. Lucy on December 13 in Sweden.

St. Nicholas, a kindly Fourth Century bishop, is the patron saint of children, sailors, marriageable maidens and pawnbrokers. The last two roles are connected: Nicholas once gave three bags of gold as dowries for three daughters of a poor man; the bags, stylized as golden balls, became the pawnbroker's emblem.

St. Lucy, who died in 304, was a devout Sicilian girl who made a vow of chastity. Her rejected suitor denounced her as a Christian, and Diocletian's soldiers killed her. Her feast is celebrated with blazing candles.

14

THE DEATH OF ST. NICHOLAS *follows a scene show-*
ing him rescuing three condemned innocents. Many
shrines were built in his honor in medieval England.

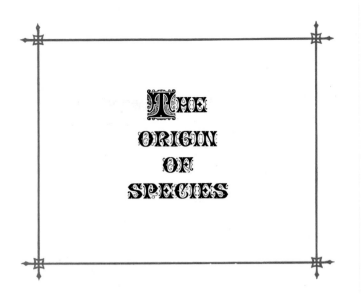

THE
ORIGIN
OF
SPECIES

The Fourth Century St. Nicholas was a modest man who did good deeds in secret. This poem by Phyllis McGinley points out how his popular image has been changed over the centuries.

Nicholas, Bishop of Myra's See,
Was holy a saint
As a saint could be;
Saved not a bit
Of his worldly wealth
And loved to commit
Good deeds by stealth.

Was there a poor man,
Wanting a roof?
Nicholas sheltered him weatherproof.
Who lacked a morsel
Had but to ask it
And at his doorsill
Was Nicholas' basket.

O, many a basket did he carry!
Penniless girls
Whom none would marry
Used to discover to their delight,
Into their windows
Tossed at night
(When the moon was old
And the dark was showery),
Bags of gold
Enough for a dowery.

People, I read,
Grew slightly lyrical,
Calling each deed
He did, a miracle.
Told how he calmed the sea for sailors

And rescued children
From awful jailors
Who, drawing lots
For the foul design,
Liked pickling tots
In pickle-brine.

Nicholas, *circa*
Fourth cent. A. D.,
Died in the odor of sanctity.
But fortune changes,
Blessings pass,
And look what's happened to Nicholas.

He who had feared
The world's applause,
Now, with a beard,
Is Santa Claus.
A multiplied elf, he struts and poses,
Ringing up sales
In putty noses;
With Comet and Cupid
His constant partners,
Telling tall tales to kindergart'ners,
His halo fickle as
Wind and wave.

While dizzily Nicholas
Spins in his grave.

St. Lucy's
Plea

St. Lucy, a Fourth Century martyr who is honored at Christmas, dedicates herself to piety in this scene by Jacobus de Voragine (1230-1298).

"Mother, now thou art cured and healthy, I pray thee for my sake whose prayers healed thee, never to suggest to me that I take a husband nor spouse, but with the dowry that thou wouldst give me, I pray thee to give it to me for alms, so that I may come unto my savior Jesus Christ." Her mother answered, "Fair daughter I have not decreased thy patrimony which I received nine years ago when thy father died, but I have multiplied and increased it. But wait until I am departed out of this world and then do as it shall please thee." Lucy replies: "After thou art dead thou may not use thy goods. . . . Give them for God's sake while thee live, every day give of thy goods."

Hodie Christus Natus Est

"Hodie Christus Natus Est" ("This day Christ is Born") is a Gregorian chant of the Seventh Century which is sung at Vespers on Christmas Day.

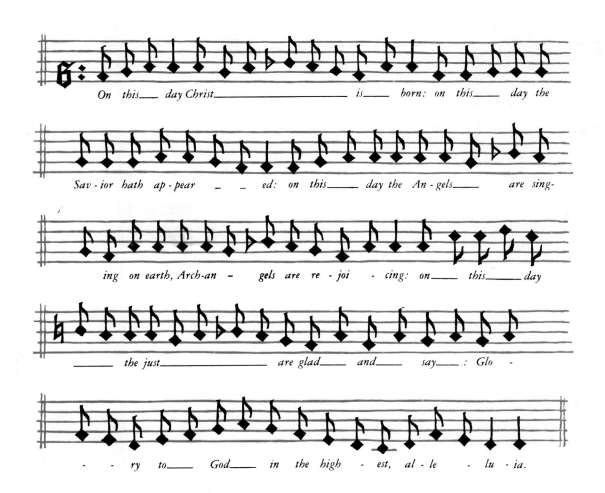

On this___ day Christ_____ is___ born: on this___ day the Sav-ior hath ap-pear _ _ ed: on this___ day the An-gels___ are sing-ing on earth, Arch-an - gels are re-joi - cing: on___ this___ day _____ the just_____ are glad___ and___ say___.: Glo - - ry to___ God___ in the high - est, al-le - lu-ia.

II

A MILITANT FAITH

HEAP ON MORE WOOD!—THE wind is chill; But let it whistle as it will, We'll keep our Christmas merry still. Each age has deemed the new-born year The fittest time for festal cheer: Even, heathen yet, the savage Dane, At Iol more deep the mead did drain; High on the beach his galleys drew, And feasted all his pirate crew; Then in his low and pine-built hall, Where shields and axes decked the wall, They gorged upon the half-dressed steer; Caroused in seas of sable beer; While round, in brutal jest, were thrown The half-gnawed rib, and marrow-bone; Or listened all, in grim delight, While scalds yelled out the joys of fight. Then forth, in frenzy, would they hie, While wildly loose their red locks fly, And, dancing round the blazing pile, They make such barbarous mirth the while, As best might to the mind recall The boisterous joys of Odin's hall.

"MARMION," SIR WALTER SCOTT

DEVOUT KING EDGAR, *shown flanked by Mary and St. Peter, offers Christ the charter of an English abbey he refounded in 966.*

RITES AND REVELS OF THE CONQUERORS

AN ANCIENT ROUND TABLE, *reputedly used by King Arthur and his knights, now hangs from a wall in England's Winchester Castle.*

DURING the early Middle Ages, roughly from the Fifth Century through the 11th Century, the celebration of Christmas was radically changed by the same mighty forces that were reshaping European history. Hordes of pagan warriors swept out of the North and East, occupying rich lands in their path. Meanwhile Christianity had grown from a missionary sect into a politically powerful institution. Its influence spread from the churches and monasteries into the strongholds of the conquerors. Increasing numbers of these rough fighting men were converted to the dynamic new faith. Their celebration of Christ's birthday mingled with their old pagan festivals held in December, when there was leisure between the fall harvest and the spring planting. Inevitably, many important state occasions were scheduled for Christmas, borrowing spiritual grandeur from the day and lending it crude pomp and gusto.

Few records survived the chaotic upheavals of the Fifth and Sixth Centuries, when Western Europe split into fragmentary kingdoms during the death throes of the Roman Empire. Yet as the war bands of the Angles and the Saxons overran England, there arose many legends centering on a heroic Briton who defended the Christian faith and his native soil from the invaders. He became known as King Arthur.

The myths of Arthur tell less about his age than about the ideals and attitudes that prevailed centuries later, when most of the stories were written. Probably the real Arthur was a rough captain of horsemen rather than the romantic monarch of resplendent knights. But, due largely to the *Morte d'Arthur,* the famous 15th Century epic by Sir Thomas Malory, Arthur and his Round Table became popular symbols of the whole medieval epoch.

Christmas is a portentous day in Arthurian legends. It was on Christmas Day that the miraculous event occurred which was to put young Arthur upon the vacant English throne. At the behest of Merlin the magician, the leaders of the realm gathered on the birthday of Jesus, in the hope that a sign from Him would reveal their rightful king. The sign took the form of a sword, embedded in an anvil, which only Arthur was able to withdraw. Malory also recorded (again with no support from history) that on a later Christmas, Arthur was crowned Emperor of Rome.

History records the long resistance of native Britons like Arthur, but the Anglo-Saxons ultimately established themselves in England. These Germanic peoples celebrated Christmas as lustily as their ancestors observed the pagan festivals of winter. For days on end, life was a boisterous round of singing, hunting, gambling, feasting and drinking wassail. Wassail bowls came into use; the beverage was usually ale or beer, sometimes hot and spiced, and it flowed in copious quantities. Alfred the Great, who reigned in the Ninth Century, tried to curb the excesses. But the raucous revelry continued in spite of his pious decree that the 12 days after Christmas were to be set apart for sacred observance.

In the Ninth and Tenth Centuries, much of Europe fell to the Norsemen, or Vikings, from Scandinavia. Along with the Anglo-Saxons and the Franks and Goths, these fierce Norse sea lords accepted Christianity and retained in their Christmas celebrations several customs from their common pagan past. The ceremonial boar's head, which they served with its tusks replaced and an apple in its mouth, probably harks back to Frey, the Norse god of the herds, whose symbol was the boar. The blazing yule log, center of so many superstitions, remained popular, and so did the bonfires that had been lit on the shortest day of the year to speed the return of the life-giving sun. Another remnant was the use of evergreens. The Norsemen and Anglo-Saxons continued to decorate their halls with evergreen boughs during their Christmas revels, but as the generations passed they slowly forgot that the custom had been a pagan act in defiance of the winter's power to kill.

As the Norse conquerors weakened in England, another power was rising in France—the more advanced and worldly Normans. It was not until the Norman influence came to Britain that a genuine order and formality entered the English Yuletide festival. And it was on Christmas Day in 1066 that William the Conqueror assumed England's throne, firmly establishing the Norman line. For that great occasion, William organized festivities that were lavish beyond the dreams of his roughhewn predecessors. Thus began an elegant era in the celebration of Christmas.

THE KNIGHTS OF THE ROUND TABLE *welcome gallant Sir Galahad, who is being led by old Merlin the magician to the vacant seat between Sir Launcelot and King Arthur. By the 14th Century, when this illumination appeared in an Italian manuscript, the tradition had grown that Arthur and his knights spent their Christmas season in boisterous feasting and drinking.*

CLOVIS I, *King of the Franks, is baptized along with 3,000 of his men in a ceremony on Christmas Day in 496. The dove hovering near him symbolizes the Holy Spirit.*

CHARLEMAGNE *is crowned Emperor of the Romans by Pope Leo III on Christmas Day, 800. These illustrations are from a 14th Century French historical chronicle.*

A DAY
FOR HISTORIC
EVENTS

When the earliest of court Christmases were celebrated, kings were little more than warrior chieftains and their courts were drafty halls in rude fortresses. But Christmas had already become the great day of the year for holding affairs of state. In Saxon England, for example, the leading nobles of the realm gathered at Christmas to advise and counsel the king. These conferences, called the Witenagemot, were an early forerunner of the present-day British Parliament.

In this tradition, Christmas set the stage for three pivotal events of medieval history, all of them involving the close political relationship between Church and state. In the year 496, Clovis I, pagan king of the Franks, was baptized on Christmas Day in the first real step toward the formation of the French nation. His conversion gave the Church a powerful ally; and it won for Clovis the important political support of the bishops, which helped to make him master of most of Gaul. On Christmas Day in 800, Charlemagne was crowned Emperor of the Romans as a reward for defending the Pope against efforts to depose him. And on Christmas Day of 1066, William the Conqueror assumed the English throne with the Pope's sanction. In return, William shipped to the Pope generous Christmas gifts of plunder.

WITH BOAR'S HEAD AND WASSAIL BOWL, *a crude figure from a medieval English calendar personifies the pleasures of feasting and drinking during the court's Christmas celebrations.*

THE KING OF JERUSALEM, *Baldwin of Edessa, is crowned in Bethlehem, which the First Crusade freed.*

THE LEGACY OF THE CRUSADES

In 1095, Pope Urban called for a great crusade to end the Moslem persecution of Christian pilgrims in the Holy Land. With burning zeal, armies led by famous knights set out to free their sacred shrines. The First Crusade was a fierce struggle, but its warriors finally seized Jerusalem in July 1099, and they celebrated that Christmas in Bethlehem. There, on Christmas Day the next year, Baldwin of Edessa received the crown of the Latin Kingdom of Jerusalem *(above)*. Thus, 11 centuries after the birth of Christ, His Church returned to political power at the place of His birth.

Eight Crusades followed, each of them seeking to sustain the first. The survivors returned from the Holy Land with many treasures of art and literature whose influence was felt throughout Europe. And legends based on the Crusades, such as the story of St. George and the Dragon, found their way into early plays of the Christmas season, which have enriched its celebration ever since.

STORMING JERUSALEM, *knights of the First Crusade seize the city in 1099. This 14th Century miniature and the one above are from a French manuscript.*

Christmas with Arthur

Legend holds that King Arthur spent his Christ-
mases in boisterous feasting and drinking. One
such celebration is disapprovingly described in
this account from an English chronicle of 1736.

At this time (A.D. 521) that great Monarch Arthur, with his Clergy, all his Nobility, and Soldiers,
kept *Christmas* in *York*, whither resorted to him
the prime Persons of the Neighbourhood, and spent
the latter End of *December* in Mirth, Jollity, Drinking and the Vices that are too often the Consequence
of them; so that the Representations of the old
Heathenish Feasts dedicated to Saturn were here
again revived; but the Number of Days they lasted
were doubled and amongst the wealthier Sort tre-
bled; during which Time they counted it almost a
Sin to treat of any serious Matter. Gifts are sent mu-
tually from and to one another; frequent invitations
pass betwixt Friends, and domestick Offenders are
not punished. Our Countrymen call this Jule-tide,
substituting the name of *Julius Caesar* for that of
Saturn. The Vulgar are yet persuaded that the Nativity of Christ is then celebrated, but mistakenly;
for 'tis plain they imitate the Lasciviousness of *Bac-*
chanalians, rather than the memory of *Christ,* then,
as they say, born.

OLAF
THE KING

Christmas was officially observed in Norway
for the first time by King Olaf in 995. In these
verses by Henry Wadsworth Longfellow (1807-
1882), Olaf and his Berserks, or armorless war-
riors, celebrate the day in their rough manner.

At Drontheim, Olaf the King
Heard the bells of Yule-tide ring,
    As he sat in his banquet hall,

Drinking the nut-brown ale,
With his bearded Berserks hale
    And tall.

O'er his drinking-horn, the sign
He made of the cross divine
    As he drank, and muttered his prayers;
But the Berserks evermore
Made the sign of the Hammer of Thor
    Over theirs.

Then King Olaf raised the hilt
Of iron, cross-shaped and gilt,
    And said, "Do not refuse;
Count well the gain and the loss,
Thor's hammer or Christ's cross:
    Choose!"

On the shining wall a vast
And shadowy cross was cast
    From the hilt of the lifted sword,
And in foaming cups of ale
The Berserks drank "Was-hael!
    To the Lord!"

THE BAPTISM OF CLOVIS

In the Middle Ages, Christmas was the tradi-
tional day for staging great state ceremonies.
One such event—the baptism of Clovis I, King
of the Franks, in 496—is described below in
an account by St. Gregory of Tours (538-594).

Then the Queen [St. Clotilde] sent secretly to Rémy,
Bishop of Reims, praying him to instil into her
husband's heart the word of salvation. The Bishop
came to the King, and little by little, and in private, brought him to acknowledge the true God,
Maker of heaven and earth, and to renounce his
idols, which could be of no avail to him or to
anyone.

Then said Clovis to the Bishop: "Most holy Sir,
I hear you willingly, but there is a difficulty: the
people I rule have no desire to abandon their gods.
Nevertheless I will speak to them according to the
spirit of your words." He thereupon went into the

midst of the people; but already the Divine grace had operated, and even before he opened his mouth to speak the assembly cried with one voice: "Pious King, we renounce our mortal gods, we are ready to serve the God whose immortality Rémy preaches." This news was brought to the Bishop, and overcome with joy he ordered the sacred fonts to be prepared. Rich hangings adorn the streets; the churches are hung with tapestries; the incense-clouds arise; fragrant tapers blaze on every hand; and all the baptistery is filled with a heavenly odour. Such grace did Almighty God shower upon those present, that they thought themselves transported among the joys of Paradise. The King first of all demanded baptism of the Bishop. Like a new Con-

stantine he advances to the bath which is to wash away his deep-rooted leprosy, to the new water which is to cleanse him of the stains of his past. As he came to the font the saint of God addressed him with holy eloquence: "Bow thy head in humility, O Sicamber! adore what thou hast burned, burn what thou hast adored."

Clovis, having confessed one God, all-powerful in the Sacred Trinity, was baptised in the name of the Father, and of the Son, and of the Holy Ghost, and anointed with the sign of the Cross with the holy chrism. More than three thousand men of his army were baptised after him, as also his sister Alb-fledis, who a little time after departed this life in the Lord.

Boar's Head Carol

The boar's head feast was an ancient pagan rite that became a part of the Christmas season. This 16th Century carol, still sung in a yearly boar's head festival at Oxford University, England, captures some of the flavor of the rude times when the Anglo-Saxon kings reigned.

The boar's head in hand bear I, Be-decked with bays and rose-ma-ry;

And I pray you, my mas-ters, be mer-ry, Quot es-tis in con-vi-vi-o:

Ca-put a-pri de-fe-ro, Red-dens lau-des Do-mi-no.

III

THE MEDIEVAL SPECTACLE

ST. NICHOLAS' DAY (DECEMBER 6) marked the opening of Christmas revelries. In the morning the Mayor and his fellows heard Mass and listened to a sermon by the Boy-Bishop; then, after dinner, they played solemnly at dice (a traditional part of the festival) until the Boy-Bishop arrived with a train of clerical attendants to give the town officers his blessing and be refreshed with bread and wine. . . . He was a busy man during this season dominated by the Lord of Misrule. The people of Bristol, like those of other towns, celebrated with mumming and gaming and dancing and brawls among visored rascals in dark streets. The Mayor heard sermons . . . and on Christmas Eve he issued the usual proclamation against wearing of masks, carrying weapons, and remaining in the streets without lights after curfew.

"THE YORKIST AGE," PAUL MURRAY KENDALL

BESTOWING GIFTS, *the Duc de Berry (sitting at right) celebrates at Christmas amid lavishness typical of late medieval courts.*

AN AGE
OF FESTIVE
PAGEANTRY

AN EPIPHANY CAKE *is portioned out to guests in the order decided by the child traditionally called Phebe, sitting under the table.*

THE EPOCH called the late Middle Ages (roughly from 1100 to 1500) started with Christianity dominant throughout Western Europe. And it spread a wide variety of Christmas celebrations through all levels of medieval society. The Nativity was observed with simple, pious pageants and with impressive Masses in those glorious monuments which the age built to its faith—the Gothic cathedrals. But this was an age of vivid secular pageantry as well as piety, and Christmas was also celebrated with magnificent rituals of knightly combat, with fantastic pantomimes and garish processions, with organized horseplay and boisterous ringing songfests.

For kings and nobles, Christmas was a gorgeous season. In England their feasting was heroic. At Christmas 1252, Henry III had 600 oxen slaughtered. These were served with plentiful salmon pie and roast peacock, and washed down with barrels and barrels of wine. In 1415, Henry V observed Christmas with a "glutton mass celebration" that went on for five days. For his wedding to Katherine of France during the Christmas season of 1420-1421, the gigantic menu boasted pike stuffed

with herbs, jelly colored with columbine flowers, roast porpoise, smelt, crayfish and such obscure dainties as dedells in burneaux and frument with balien.

The wassail bowl of Saxon times maintained its prominent place in this trencherman's Christmas. In one recipe the basic ingredient, ale, was liberally spiked with sugar, apples, toast and roasted crabs. Topers intended no sacrilege when they implored:

For our blyssd Lady sake,
Bryng us in good ale!

Along with gourmandizing went lavish display in dress. For Christmas in 1201, King John of England "taxed his purse and ingenuity in providing all his servitors with costly apparel," and he was much vexed when the Archbishop of Canterbury tried to outshine him.

The giving of gifts —on New Year's Day and on Christmas—was customary by the 12th Century. Kings and nobles held to a scale of presents, usually money, for those in their retinue, but the gifts they exchanged themselves were often ostentatious. In 1236 England's Henry III received a truly spectacular present from the King of France —a live elephant.

Throughout the period, gaiety and excess increased. At Christmastime Spaniards danced in churches and Englishmen gambled with special fervor. Clerical warnings against these sinful acts had scant effect. In 1497-1498 English authorities settled for a forlorn victory by banning cardplaying by apprentices *except* at the Yuletide. Among many other Christmas extravaganzas were wrestling matches and grand hunting parties *(opposite)*. Foot and horse races were held on St. Staffan's Day, the

second day of Christmas, in Sweden, Germany and elsewhere. But for sheer spectacle none of the Christmas events matched the tournaments. In these contests, elaborately staged in many parts of Western Europe, knights matched lances before large, colorful holiday crowds.

In France, the special day for frolicking was Epiphany (January 6). It was the occasion for the Feast of Fools, a pagan survival in which certain members of the lower clergy elected their own Bishop of Fools. He conducted a mock mass, and "all sorts of buffooneries and abominations were permitted." Closely akin to the Bishop of Fools were England's Boy Bishops, whose religious satires took a milder form, and also the Lords of Misrule, who were appointed by noblemen and communities to lead their Christmas festivities. Official censure put a stop to the Bishop of Fools in the 15th Century, but the other festive figures continued to hold sway.

The French Epiphany was also celebrated with the *gâteau des rois*, or cake of the Kings. In one version of it, this big confection was baked with a single bean inside and distributed by the child called Phebe *(above)*. Whoever got the bean became the ruler of the day, chose a consort and ordered dancing and games. Apparently begun by monks in the 13th Century, the custom reached court circles and then ordinary homes, in some of which it is still observed.

By the end of the epoch, court Christmases could scarcely become more extravagant. Even the modest homes in England held elaborate festivities, while on the streets at night the minstrels and the poor and the mocking Lords of Misrule celebrated with roisterous merriment.

ON A CHRISTMAS HUNT, *spear-bearing nobles with their dogs pursue a boar (left) in this painting from an illuminated French manuscript of the 15th Century. The boar had been the symbol of a pagan deity centuries before. In later Christmas celebrations, the boar's head feast became associated with the court, and the boar hunt was a sport traditionally reserved for lords.*

PERFORMANCES TO GREET THE SEASON

POSING AS A BIBLICAL KING, *Charles VII of France is depicted presenting a gift to the Christ child in this Adoration scene painted by Jean Fouquet, a French court artist of the 15th Century.*

WEARING ANIMAL HEADS, *three mummers (below) cavort in this picture from a 14th Century manuscript. Such pantomimists also performed as dragons, peacocks and satyrlike wild men.*

Christmas in the late Middle Ages brought out a host of festive performers. By the mid-1100s, costumed maskers, or mummers, began appearing in the English court, where they acted out gay, fanciful pantomimes. Sometimes they dressed as animals *(left, below)* or as various fantastic creatures. The minstrels—a motley crew of actors, singers and jugglers—performed for coins in the taverns as well as the courts. To program all of their entertainments, kings and nobles often required their own special directors. These chief celebrants were called, appropriately, Lords of Misrule; and in a pagan tradition that dated to the Roman Saturnalia festival, they gleefully overturned the social order for the long Christmas season.

Even kings had their fling at festive masquerading. The occasion was Three Kings Day, which occurred on Epiphany, January 6. Celebrated in honor of the three Biblical Kings, this festival gradually became a major holiday in France and Spain. At Paris in 1378 three monarchs, including Charles V of France, attended Mass richly costumed as the Biblical Kings. A number of rulers posed for portraits in their disguise *(left)*.

The most important type of medieval performance was the drama. On the Continent, the only early drama was a simple, pious Christmas pageant which dramatized the birth of Jesus. It was variously known as the Nativity play, the miracle play, the mystery play. But in England another pageant, as simple as the Nativity play but more worldly in content, was also performed at Christmas. This was *St. George and the Dragon*, which dramatized the many legends of England's patron saint *(opposite)*. These representatives of two dramatic traditions, the religious and the secular, survived side by side for centuries, developing a store of dramatic knowledge that later contributed to the Elizabethan theater.

BATTLING THE DRAGON, *St. George (opposite) aims a deathblow in this 15th Century painting. The St. George legends grew up around a soldier who turned Christian and died as a martyr.*

De sancto georgio ã.   cepisset uenerunt capa

Cum autem beat'   docie regionis uiri excel

georgius in no   lentissimi et sanctium

mine dei martinum re   corpus eius nocturno

ENGLAND'S KING JOHN, *shunned as a despot, broods alone with his dogs. At Christmas 1214 he was served with demands that led to the Magna Charta.*

A TIME
FOR TILTING
AND
CHIVALRY

The tournament, that public testing of knightly vows and valor, was the grandest of medieval displays; and many of the greatest tourneys were held at Christmastime. Richard the Lionhearted, brother of John *(above)* and a hero of the Age of Chivalry, was a flamboyant champion of the joust. One story tells that on Christmas Day, 1190, while he was leading the Third Crusade to a real war in the Holy Land, Richard paused in Sicily to stage a mock war. His powerful knights armed themselves with reeds, then joined the fray. To the victors Richard gave rich prizes.

Two centuries later, the second Richard of England presented a particularly dazzling Christmas tourney. Champions from all over Western Europe came to compete. On opening day, heralds and minstrels accompanied 65 steeds through London to the lists. Then came 60 elegant horsewomen, each one leading a knight in dramatic regalia. The warrior brotherhood splintered many a lance in their ritual of violence. After awards were made, the court returned to a sumptuous feast and a night of dancing. The whole lavish pageant was repeated daily for almost two weeks.

IN CEREMONIOUS COMBAT *before their fair ladies, knights clash with lances (left), while lesser men hurl spears and stones for distance. Such tourneys were the most spectacular of medieval Christmas events. The jousting riders shown above decorate a 15th Century chronicle.*

35

NEW MODES FOR MESSAGES OF FAITH

As the Middle Ages wore on, the celebration of Christmas moved slowly but steadily away from the Church. Miracle plays, which combined entertainment with moral lessons *(opposite),* drew enthusiastic audiences. From the 14th Century on, the solemn Latin hymns of the Church were joined by music in a vivacious new style. In the new music, the melodies were based on dance rhythms and the words were sung in the native language of the land. They were carols from England, shepherds' songs from Germany and noels from France. They spoke of the personal side of the Nativity—the mother, the Babe, the animals and the love of God for His children.

These sentiments, too, moved St. Francis of Assisi, who loved all animals and often preached to the birds *(left).* Seeking to bring home to people the joyful message of Christ's birth, the gentle friar built a life-sized crèche of the Nativity. The crib succeeded beyond his fondest hopes, winning wide popularity in his own time.

LOVE AND DEVOTION *bring St. Francis of Assisi into the fields to address the birds and the animals as his friends. This 14th Century stained-glass window is in a former monastery in Königsfelden, Switzerland.*

HORROR AND DROLLERY *are combined in this 15th Century illustration of a miracle play. It depicts graceful angels battling a band of weird devils for possession of the Castle of Faith.*

Cy commence le ·v̊· et deienier liuie de ce present volume intitule / La for
tresse de la foy ·

vᵉ· et deienier liuie de ce present
volume experimenter quelq chose
la force des diables peut contre icel
le nostre fortresse de la foy · Et ad
fin que ie puisse expliquer le con
cenement de ma pensee ·xij· consi
derations me viennent au deuant
en lentendement a traittier touchāt

pres que nous
auons demôstre
comment les bat
tailles des nuytz
et des sarrazins
gnesuent peu a
nostre fortresse de la foy il reste en ce

AN ELABORATE CRADLE, *probably used at Christmas to rock a figurine of the infant Jesus, is a 15th Century rarity from Germany.*

THE SPREAD OF HOLIDAY CUSTOMS

As medieval society grew more complex, the secular and the religious tended to merge in the celebration of Christmas. The crèche was often built in the town by lay organizations like the craft guilds; yet just as often the same groups, as parishioners, built the crib in the church. Carol singing, another of the age's original contributions to Christmas, was born in part as a reaction to the grave theology of Church music in Latin; yet in time these lively carols were also sung, in the vernacular, in monastery cloisters. Minstrels *(opposite)*, roving farther afield as travel grew safer and easier, made the same tunes favorites in many places. With the age's slow growth of commerce and its accelerating exchange of fresh ideas, no Christmas tradition died for the lack of exposure. In southern Germany the *Kindelwiegen (above)*, a cradle designed for a figurine of the Christ child, remained a local custom simply because it had limited appeal.

The new spirit which animated Christmastime heralded a new age —the Renaissance. In the Renaissance spirit of adventure an Italian captain sailing for Spain signaled the closing of the Middle Ages. And it was on Christmas Eve of 1492 that Columbus' cockleshell flagship ran aground on a reef in the New World.

A SCHOOL FOR MINSTRELS *rehearses before a teacher in this German illustration of the 14th Century. By then, such licensed vagabonds were spreading their gaiety throughout Europe.*

38

THE MISTAKE OF COLUMBUS

Marco Polo named Japan "Cipangu." When Columbus' ship ran aground in the New World on Christmas Eve, 1492, he believed he had found Japan. This excerpt is from his ship's log.

MONDAY: DECEMBER 24TH

Before sunrise, he weighed anchor with a land breeze. Among the many Indians who had come yesterday to the ship and who had indicated to them that there was gold in that island and had named the places where it was collected, he saw one who seemed to be better disposed and more attached to him, or who spoke to him with more pleasure. He flattered this man and asked him to go with him to show him the mines of gold. This Indian brought another, a friend or relation, with him, and among the other places which they named where gold was found, they spoke of Cipangu, which they call "Cibao," and they declared that there was a great quantity of gold there, and that the cacique carries banners of beaten gold, but that it is very far to the east. The admiral here says these words to the Sovereigns: "Your Highnesses may believe that in all the world there cannot be a people better or more gentle. Your Highnesses should feel great joy, because they will presently become Christians, and will be educated in the good customs of your realms, for there cannot be a better people or country...."

The Dragon Killer

St. George, England's patron saint, lived in the Near East and never saw England. But in this passage from a medieval Christmas play he is called a Briton—and also a prince of Egypt.

Enter Father Christmas.
Here come I, old Father Christmas,
    Welcome, or welcome not,
I hope old Father Christmas
    Will never be forgot.
I am not come here to laugh or to jeer,
But for a pocketfull of money, and a skinfull of beer,
If you will not believe what I do say,

Come in the King of Egypt—clear the way.
Enter the King of Egypt.
Here I, the King of Egypt, boldly do appear,
St. George, St. George, walk in, my only son and heir.
Walk in, my son St. George, and boldly act thy part,
That all the people here may see thy wond'rous art.
Enter Saint George.
Here come I, St. George, from Britain did I spring,
I'll fight the Dragon bold, my wonders to begin.
I'll clip his wings, he shall not fly;
I'll cut him down, or else I die.
Enter the Dragon.
Who's he that seeks the Dragon's blood,
And calls so angry, and so loud?
That English dog, will he before me stand?
I'll cut him down with my courageous hand.
With my long teeth, and scurvy jaw,
Of such I'd break up half a score,
And stay my stomach, till I'd more.

The Decline of the Joust

Christmas jousting kept the knights and their ladies in a gay mood. "The Shorter Cambridge Medieval History," in the paragraphs below, shows how the blood sport became relatively safe.

The typical sport of chivalry from the eleventh century, if not earlier in some form, was the mimic warfare of the tournament. The two main varieties, usually seen on the same occasion, were the joust or single combat with lance and sword, and the *mêlée* when two opposed parties fought. They were frequent and popular in the twelfth century; a skilful knight could support himself on the ransoms of those he vanquished. But the loss of life and limb in these murderous conflicts led the Church to condemn them under pain of excommunication of the participants. The Lateran Council of 1179 denied Christian burial to the slain. The effect, however, of these canons was small enough, although a steady tendency was shown from the thirteenth century towards lessening the danger by the use of blunted weapons. They gradually became more ceremonial and artificial. In the fifteenth century the *mêlée* almost disappeared, and the joust was mostly a test of skill in unhorsing an adversary with all precautions against collisions of the chargers and the like. Even so, sharp weapons might be used and men be killed outright. In Germany it was necessary for the jousters in these noble sports to prove ancestry unblemished by recent mésalliance. In general the tournament by these restrictions be-

came more and more divorced from actual warfare, but in fact in its cruder form it had already lost touch with the advance of military science. To counter the long-bow, indeed, the knight's armour had been much developed. Breast-plates and leg-armour of plate or leather had been added to chain mail, and the fifteenth-century complete suit of plate steel as well as the armoured horse were well in sight, but the result was cumbrous to a degree; the knight thrown to the ground was nearly helpless.

Coventry Carol

Nativity plays were often staged by medieval craft guilds.
In 1534, the Shearmen and Tailors' Guild of Coventry
incorporated this Christmas carol in their famous play.

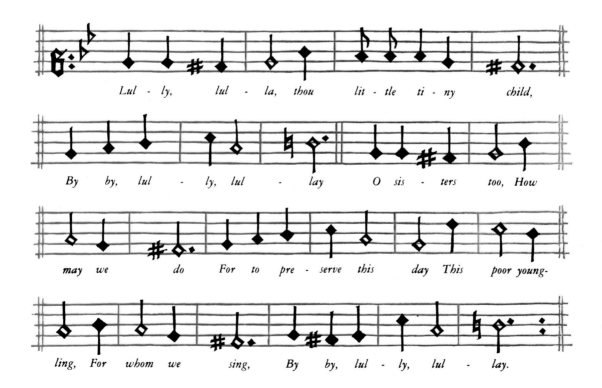

Lul - ly, lul - la, thou lit - tle ti - ny child,
By by, lul - ly, lul - lay O sis - ters too, How
may we do For to pre - serve this day This poor young-
ling, For whom we sing, By by, lul - ly, lul - lay.

IV

IN AND OUT OF FAVOR

ALL THE...HARMELESSE SPORTS, with the merry Gambolls, dances and friscolls, which the toyling Plowswaine, and Labourer, once a yeare were wont to be recreated, and their spirits and hopes reviv'd for a whole twelve month, are now extinct and put out of use, in such a fashion as if they never had bin. Thus are the merry Lords of misrule, supprest by the mad Lords of bad rule at Westminster. And to roast a Surloyn of Beefe, to touch a Collar of Brawne, to bake a Pye, to put a plumb in the pottadge pot, to burne a great Candle, or to lay one blocke the more in the fire for your sake (Master *Christmas*) is enough to make a man to be suspected and taken for a Christian, for which he shall be apprehended for committing high Parliament-Treason...

"THE COMPLAINT OF CHRISTMAS," JOHN TAYLOR

A GAY TREE *is paraded in a German square. This 16th Century painting is one of the earliest to show the Christmas tree custom.*

A BRIGHT
SEASON
BANISHED

HENRY VIII OF ENGLAND, *renowned for his Christmastime feasting, is depicted in this miniature with his jester, Will Somers.*

LUSTY AND PROUD, Henry VIII ascended the throne of England in 1509. By then, explorer John Cabot had staked England's claim to a New World empire. Henry, the epitome of the Renaissance king, was alert to the promises of exploration and prodigious in his appetite for life. His court functions and Christmas celebrations had an assured majesty that outshone his predecessors'. Of Henry's Twelfth Night festival in 1512, a court historian wrote: "at night, the King with XI others, wer disguised after the maner of Italie, called a maske, a thing not seen afore in England." After the banquet, "maskers came in with six gentlemen disguised in silke, bearing staffe torches, and desired the ladies to daunce." This elegant caprice was a masked ball, a glittering addition to Christmas.

In their city homes or country manors, noblemen and gentry created their own magnificence. Many of them kept "a maker of Interludes" to compose the yearly entertainments. Most of them employed as director of their festivities a Master of Revels or—continuing an older and wilder tradition—a Lord of Misrule. The clergy still had their revels too—the upside-down days when a Boy Bishop ruled. But in 1541,

Henry VIII banned Boy Bishops, and a few decades later, the Lords of Misrule began to fade.

By 1541, the Reformation had begun. Luther had founded his Church. John Calvin was establishing his Calvinist, or Presbyterian, Church in Geneva. And, in 1534, Henry VIII had assumed control of the Church in England. Luther, though a reformer, was no puritan. He enjoyed the festival of Christmas, adding to it hymns of his own and, according to legend, the Christmas tree. Although the legend is more generous than accurate, it was among Lutherans that the tree first became a Christmas tradition. The earliest written record of a fully decorated Christmas tree dates from 1605, when a citizen of Strasbourg wrote that "at Christmas they set up fir trees in the parlors . . . and hang upon them roses cut from many-colored paper, apples, wafers, gilt-sugar, sweets, etc."

In England the Reformation did not immediately alter Christmas. But Christmas was being considerably changed by the sophistication of the Renaissance. The old, pious Nativity plays, which seemed coarse and superstitious to the worldly Renaissance man, were steadily dwindling. By the end of the century, they were seldom performed in England, and a new drama, complex and humanistic, was in full flower.

At the court on Christmas of 1594, the new drama brought together its leading patron and playwright—Queen Elizabeth and William Shakespeare. As an actor, Shakespeare often performed for Elizabeth and his plays remained a popular court attraction after James I succeeded her. During James's second Christmas season as king in 1604-1605, seven of Shakespeare's plays and two of Ben Jonson's were

performed. In that season too, the first great Christmas masque was seen: Jonson's *Masque of Blackness.* It was a splendid blend of masquerade and music, and Inigo Jones, the finest stage architect of the day, produced it magnificently. It cost £3,000.

Puritans were shocked by such extravagance, and also by Christmas itself, which seemed to them dangerously pagan. One Puritan angrily noted that "in Christmas tyme there is nothing else used but cardes, dice, tables, maskyng, mumming, bowling, and suche like fooleries." In 1642 the Puritans came to power in England, and under Oliver Cromwell the streets of London resounded to the town criers' shouts of "No Christmas! No Christmas!" Playhouses were shut; the day of feasting was turned into a fast. When Londoners decked their streets with greenery, the Lord Mayor had the boughs all burned. Citizens were expected to report to work as usual, and Parliament declared that on the day "commonly called Christmas, no observance shall be had, nor any solemnity used or exercised in churches in respect thereof."

This severe attitude toward Christmas prevailed in New England too. The Pilgrims, who had started building their Plymouth colony on Christmas Day in 1620, still shunned the holiday in favor of hard work. The Puritans in the Massachusetts Bay Colony were threatened with a five-shilling fine for "observing any such day as Christmas." Throughout Cromwell's government, planters in the American South continued to celebrate their courtly Christmas. But even after Cromwell's downfall brought Christmas back to England, the holiday retained its solemn tone in most of Puritan New England.

A SPIRITED COUPLE, *Queen Elizabeth and the Earl of Leicester leap in a lively and informal dance. Elizabeth's Christmas entertainments also included masked dances and pantomimes, and she ordered court productions of tragedies, comedies and historical chronicles. Actor William Shakespeare often performed in these plays. This 16th Century painting hangs in Penshurst Place.*

THE MAGICAL WORLD OF MASQUES

AN ORNATE STAGE-SET *for a Christmas masque represents the façade of a palace. This design by Inigo Jones was drawn for Ben Jonson's "Oberon." The masque was first performed in 1611.*

Dramatist Ben Jonson was the master of the new form of courtly theater, the masque, and in the reign of King James his entertainments were frequently produced on Twelfth Night. Inigo Jones, England's first great architect, staged and costumed Jonson's masques. The result was both intelligent allegory and sumptuous show. Court people and events in their lives were often represented and celebrated in these masques. The *Masque of Hymen,* which Jonson wrote in honor of the marriage of the 13-year-old daughter of the Lord Chamberlain to the 14-year-old Earl of Essex, was acted in the Christmas season of 1606. Declared one guest, "I think they hired and borrowed all the principal jewels and ropes of pearls both in Court or city." At the end of the great performance, the women in the cast chose partners from the audience and the men performers "gleaned out the Queen, the bride, and the greatest of the ladies." And then they all danced.

FANTASTIC ATTIRE *for characters in "Oberon" (above) demonstrates the splendor and imagination of a regal age. The sketches are by Inigo Jones.*

A WINGED SPRITE NAMED IRIS, *from Jonson's "Masque of Hymen," hovers airily in another of Jones's sketches. The stage was banked with artificial clouds from which dancers descended.*

A TWELFTH NIGHT FEAST *is merrily celebrated in this painting by the 17th Century Dutch artist, Jan Steen. The child wearing the crown became king of the holiday by finding the one bean in his Christmas cake. Steen often portrayed the lively pleasures of Holland's rising middle class.*

HAPPY CELEBRATIONS IN THE HOME

Christmas was celebrated in 17th Century homes with a liberality based on new wealth. The fine feasts and prosperous families pictured by the Dutch painter Jan Steen give evidence of the abundance enjoyed by Holland's middle classes. Elsewhere in Europe, colonial trade and home industry enlarged a new class whose interests were commercial and whose pleasures were domestic.

The stage for their celebrations was the home. The importance of children in the Christmas season was increasing. As the paintings shown here suggest, the young were often the center of festivities.

One of the family's most popular Twelfth Night festivities was the choosing of the King of the Bean. Traditionally, the bean was hidden in a cake; the finder became monarch of the night, chose a queen and ordered the court to drink or dance. Since Twelfth Night concluded the season, it often produced marathon revels. On one such occasion, the English diarist Samuel Pepys saw the bean king chosen in his home, then recorded that he wearily retired, "leaving my wife and people at their sports, which they continued till morning, not coming to bed at all."

ST. NICHOLAS' GIFTS, *found in the shoes in this Dutch scene, delight a good girl and sadden the bad boy who got only a switch. The basket on the floor contains St. Nicholas' Eve cakes.*

A BAND OF CHERUBS *encircles this cast of a Christmas dough-mold from Germany. The center scene shows Jesus turning water into wine. Cakes were baked in such molds only on the holiday.*

SPECIAL
HOLIDAY ARTISTRY

Christmas joy in the 17th Century was richly expressed in the ornaments and housewares that families brought out to welcome the glad season. Rooms were decorated with greenery and the walls were hung with bright tapestries like the Nor-

wegian one shown on the opposite page. Traditional holiday foods were prepared. Cakes were made in ornate molds *(above)*. In France, Christmas cakes were formed in the shape of animals or men; a piece of the cake was said to be able to cure the sick.

In Scandinavia, Yule Boar bread was baked and some of it was set aside and mixed with seed in the belief it helped to make crops grow. Thus old customs combined with new festivities to make Christmas as cheerful at home as it was lavish in court.

A VARIETY OF COLORS *dramatizes the Adoration of the Magi in this brilliant 17th Century Norwegian tapestry. Hangings like this were used to bedeck the halls at Christmastime.*

SHAKESPEARE'S GIFT TO GOOD QUEEN BESS

In this excerpt from a story by Anna Benne-son McMahan (1846-1919), a play by Shake-speare is presented at Christmas for Elizabeth I.

The numberless diamond-shaped window panes of the Mermaid Tavern are twinkling like so many stars in the chill December air of London. It is the last meeting of the Mermaid Club for the year 1596, and not a member is absent. As they drop in by twos and threes and gather in groups about the room, it is plain that expectation is on tip-toe. . . . Some are young, handsome, fastidious in person and dress; others are bohemian in costume, speech, and action; all wear knee breeches, and nearly all have pointed beards. He of the harsh fighting face, of the fine eye and coarse lip and the shaggy hair, whom they call Ben, although one of the youngest is yet plainly one of the leaders both for wit and for wisdom.

That grave and handsome gentleman whose lordly bearing and princely dress mark his high rank, is another favourite. He has written charming poems, has fought gallantly on many fields, has voyaged widely on many seas, has founded colonies in distant America, is a favourite of the Queen. But in this Mermaid Club his chief glory is that he is its founder and leader, the one whose magnetism and personal charm have summoned and cemented in friendship all these varied elements.

At last the all-important matter of the yearly Christmas play at court has been settled; the Master of the Revels has chosen from the rich stores of his manuscripts *The Midsummer Night's Dream*, graciously adding that "for wit and mirth it is like to please her Majesty exceedingly." A high honor, indeed, for its author. . . .

For now the successful candidate is one of the youngest and best beloved of this jolly coterie, and their pride in him is shown by the eagerness with which they await his coming to read to them the changes in the manuscript of his play since its former presentation. Ah! hear the burst of applause that greets his late arrival—a high-browed, sandy-haired man of thirty-two, lithe in figure, of middle height, with a smile of great sweetness, yet sad withal. On his face, one may read the lines of recent sorrow, and all know that he has returned but re-

cently to London from the mournful errand which took him to his Stratford home—the burial of his dearly beloved and only son, Hamnet. The plaudits for the author of the most successful play of the season—*Romeo and Juliet* . . .—were little heeded by the grief-stricken father as he urged his horse over the rough roads of the four days' journey, arriving just too late for a parting word from dying lips. But private sorrows are not for those who are called to public duties; a writer must trim his pen not to his own mood, but to the mood of the hour. And Queen Elizabeth, old in years, but ever young in her love of fun and frolic and flattery, must be made to forget the heaviness of time and the infirmities of age. If she may no longer take part in outdoor sports—the hunting, the hawking, the bearbaiting—she still may command processions, fetes, masques, and stage-plays. It pleases her now to see this wonderful fairy piece, of which she has heard so much since, two years ago, it graced the nuptials of the Earl of Derby. Does she not remember also that pretty impromptu verse of the author when acting the part of King in another man's play, two years ago at Greenwich? Did she not twice drop her glove near his feet in crossing the stage? . . . And how happily had he responded to the challenge! True to the character as well as to the metre of his part, he had picked up the glove, presenting it to its owner with the words:—"And though now bent on this high embassy, Yet stoope we to take up our cousin's glove."

It is Christmas night. Lords, ladies, and ambassadors have been summoned to Whitehall Palace to witness the play for which author, actors, and artists of many kinds have been working so industriously during the past few weeks. The Banqueting Hall, with a temporary stage at one end, has been converted into a fine auditorium.

Facing the stage, and beneath her canopy of state, sits Queen Elizabeth, in ruff and farthingale, her hair loaded with crowns and powdered with diamonds, while her sharp smile and keen glance take note of every incident. Nearest her person and evidently the chief favourite of the moment, is the man who has long been considered the Adonis of the Court. He is now also its hero, having but recently returned from the wars in Spain, where his gallantry and promptitude at Cadiz have won new glories for Her Majesty. In five short years more, his head will come to the block by decree of this same Majesty; but this no one can foresee and all voices now unite in praises for the brave and generous Essex.

nother conspicuous favourite is a blue-eyed, pink-cheeked young fellow of twenty-three, whose scarcely perceptible beard and moustache, and curly auburn hair falling over his shoulders and halfway to his waist, would suggest femininity except for his martial manner and tall figure. His resplendent attire is notable even in this gorgeously arrayed company. His white satin doublet has a broad collar, edged with lace and embroidered with silver thread; the white trunks and knee breeches are laced with gold; the sword belt, embroidered in red and gold, is decorated at intervals with white silk bows; purple garters, embroidered in silver thread, fasten the white stockings below the knee. As one of the handsomest of Elizabeth's courtiers, and also one of the most distinguished for birth, wealth, and wit, he would be a striking figure at any time; but tonight he has the added distinction of being the special friend and munificent patron of the author of the play that they have come to witness. To him had been dedicated the author's first appeal to the reading public—a poem called "Venus and Adonis," published some three years since; also, a certain "sugared sonnet," privately circulated, protesting—

> For to no other pass my verses tend
> Than of your graces and your gifts to tell.

And through the patronage of this man—the gracious Earl of Southampton—the actor-author was first brought to the Queen's notice, finally leading to the present distinction at her hands.

But now the stage compels attention. The silk curtains are withdrawn, disclosing a setting of such elaboration and illusion as never before has been witnessed by sixteenth century eyes. Never before has the frugal Elizabeth consented to such an expenditure for costumes, properties, lights, and music. In vain the audience awaits the coming of the author; he is behind the scenes, an anxious and watchful partner with the machinist in securing the proper working of these new mechanical appliances, and the smoothness of the scene shifting. The Queen is a connoisseur in these matters, and there must be no bungling. . . .

he Christmas play is over, but not over the Christmas fun. Lords and ladies are but human, and have devised a "stately dance," in which they themselves participate until nearly sunrise, the Queen herself joining at times, and never so happy as when assured of her "wondrous majesty and grace."

EVELYN'S ARREST

Cromwell's Puritan hatred of the "popery" of Christmas is vividly described below in a selection from the diary of John Evelyn (1620-1706).

25 I went to London with my Wife, to celebrate Christmas-day, Mr. Gunning preaching . . . as he was giving us ye Holy Sacrament, the chapell was surrounded with souldiers, and all the communicants and assembly surpriz'd and kept prisoners by them, some in the house, others carried away. It fell to my share to be confin'd to a roome in the house, where yet I was permitted to dine with the master of it, ye Countesse of Dorset, Lady Hatton, and some others of quality who invited me. In the afternoone came Col. Whaley, Goffe, and others, from White-hall, to examine us one by one. . . . When I came before them they tooke my name and abode, examin'd me why, contrary to an ordinance made that none should any longer observe ye superstitious time of the Nativity (so esteem'd by them), I durst offend, and particularly be at Common Prayers, which they told me was but ye masse in English, and particularly pray for Charles Steuart, for which we had no Scripture. I told them we did not pray for Cha. Steuart, but for all Christian Kings, Princes, and Governors. They replied, in so doing we praied for the K. of Spaine too, who was their enemie and a papist, with other frivolous and insnaring questions and much threatning; and finding no colour to detaine me, they dismiss'd me with much pitty of my ignorance. These were men of high flight and above ordinances, and spakeful things of our Lord's Nativity. As we went up to receive the Sacrament the miscreants held their muskets against us as if they would have shot us. . . .

Christmas with Pepys

A domestic Christmas in London, both devout and quietly festive, is described in this entry from the diary of Samuel Pepys (1633-1703). It is 1666, the year of the great London fire.

25 Christmas day Lay pretty long in bed, and then rose, leaving my wife desirous to sleep, having sat up till four this morning seeing her mayds make mince pies. I to church, where our parson Mills made a good sermon. Then home, and dined on some good ribbs of beef roasted and mince pies; only my wife, brother, and Barker, and plenty of good wine of my owne, and my heart full of true joy; and thanks to God Almighty for the goodness of my condition at this day. After dinner, I begun to teach my wife and Barker my song, "It is decreed," which pleases me mightily as now I have Mr. Hinxton's base. Then out and walked alone on foot to the Temple, it being a fine frost, thinking to have seen a play all alone; but there, missing of any bills, concluded there was none, and so back home; and there with my brother reducing the names of all my books to an alphabet, which kept us till 7 or 8 at night, and then to supper, W. Hewer with us, and pretty merry, and then to my chamber to enter this day's journal only. . . .

Christmas Banned

The Puritan ban on all Christmas celebrations was enforced in the New World by the Massachusetts Bay Colony in this decree reprinted from its legislative record of May 11, 1659.

For pventing disorders arising in seuerall places wthn this jurisdiccon, by reason of some still observing such ffestiualls as were superstitiously kept in other countrys, to the great dishonnor of God & offence of others, it is therefore ordered by this Court and the authority thereof, that whosoeuer shall be found observing any such day as Christmas or the like, either by forbearing of labour, feasting, or any other way, vpon any such accounts as aforesajd, euery such person so offending shall pay for euery such offence fiue shillings, as a find to the county. And whereas, not only at such tjmes, but at seuerall other tjmes also, it is a custome too frequent in many places to expend time in vnlawfull games, as cards, dice &c, it is therefore futher ordered, and by the Court declared, that, after publication hereof, whosoeuer shall be found in any place wthin this jurisdiccon playing either at cards or at dice, contrary to this order, shall pay as a fine to the county the some of fiue shillings for euy such offence.

TWELFTH NIGHT WITH FRANCIS

"The Gentleman of Renaissance France" contains this description of the wild court fêtes in France under King Francis I (1494-1547).

The King and his retinue, after having made a little sojourn at Amboise around Christmas, went on north a few miles to spend the *fête des Rois* (or Twelfth Night) of 1521 at Romorantin. It all started when the news came to Francis that the Comte de Saint-Pol in his house nearby had just chosen a king for the festival: some courtier had already by chance found in the Twelfth Night cake the large bean that made him king for the day, a gay ceremony that is still done in France on the sixth of January. The King, in high good spirits, decided "with the young gentlemen of his court" to challenge the authority of this king that had got his crown so easily. Saint-Pol and a group in his domain accepted the challenge, and laid in a supply of ammunition to defend the temporarily royal castle against the besiegers. The defense material consisted of a "prodigious quantity of snowballs, eggs, and apples," which turned out not to be enough to repel the assault, for the attackers were soon pushing in the doors and the ammunition was all gone. In the excitement, someone snatched a burning chunk of wood from a fireplace upstairs and threw it out a window. It struck the King on the side of the head, wounding him quite seriously. Nevertheless, he would permit no investigations to be made as to who had thrown the almost deadly missile, saying that if he indulged in such tomfoolery, he would have to take his chances on any accident. . . . It seems likely that the episode caused the King to have a permanent scar . . . which he covered with a beard—and thus popularized beards at Court.

INDIAN EPIPHANY

Father Jean Enjalran, a Jesuit missionary in Canada, reveals the childlike piety of many Indian converts in his 1679 account of an Epiphany celebration from the "Jesuit Relations."

All our savages, but especially the hurons, profess to have a special esteem for the all-endearing mystery of the birth of our lord Jesus Christ. I have seen some notable proofs of this given by these latter; they themselves entreated the father, long before the feast-day, to make arrangements so as to celebrate it in the most solemn manner possible. They sent their children to seek for what could be used in constructing a grotto, in which they were to make a representation of the mystery; and I took pleasure in hearing a little girl who, having brought with much care a beautiful sort of grass, said that she had done it in the thought and hope that the little infant Jesus might be Laid upon that grass. Our good Christians made some more serious preparations, For they all confessed; and those to whom permission was given to receive Communion, did

so very devoutly, at the midnight mass. The grotto, which was well fitted to inspire devotion, was Incessantly visited; and it rendered a very pleasing although rather protracted Service,—to draw from them the expression of their feelings as they themselves express them, when addressing the divine child. As a Climax to their devotion, they asked that the infant Jesus should do them the favor of visiting them, by being carried through their village. But, as they thought that they had rendered themselves Unworthy of this by some things that had taken place, they held grand Councils and took great precautions to obtain this favor from their missionary. The Matter was conceded to them, and carried out on the Day of the epiphany in a manner that seems to me worthy of being recorded. For my part, I was much touched by it.

They desired, then, in execution of their design, to imitate what in other ages had been done by the three great stranger Captains, who came to confess and adore Jesus Christ in the Manger, and afterward went to preach him in their own country. All the hurons, Christians and non-Christians, divided themselves into three companies, according to the different nations that constitute their village; and, after Choosing their Chiefs, one for each nation, they furnished them with porcelain, of which they were to make an offering to the infant Jesus. Every one adorned himself as handsomely as he could. The three Captains had each a scepter in his hand, to which was fastened the offering, and wore a gaudy head-dress in guise of a crown. Each company took up a different position. The signal for marching having been given them at the sound of the trumpet, they heeded the sound as that of a voice Inviting them to go to see and adore an infant God new-born. Just as the 1st company took up their march,—conducted by a star fastened to a large standard of the Color of Sky-blue, and having at the *rear* [head] their Captain, before whom was carried his banner,—The 2nd company, seeing the first marching, demanded of them [aloud] the object of their journey; and on learning it, they Joined themselves to them, having in like manner their chief at their head with his banner. The 3rd company, more advanced on the Road, did as the second; and, one after another, they continued their march, and entered our Church, the star remaining at the entrance. The 3 chiefs, having first prostrated themselves, and laid their Crowns and scepters at the feet of the infant Jesus in the Cradle, offered their Congratulations and presents to their savior. As they did so, they made a public protestation of the submission and obedience that they desired to render him; solicited faith for those who possessed it not, and protection for all their nation and for all that land; and, in conclusion, entreated him to approve that they should bring him into their village, of which they desired he should be the master. I was engaged in carrying the little statue of the divine infant, which inspired great devotion; I took it from the grotto, and from its cradle, and carried it on a fine linen cloth. Every one seemed touched, and Pressed forward in the crowd, to get a nearer view of the holy Child. Our hurons left the church in the same order in which they had come. I came after them, carrying the little statue, preceded by two frenchmen bearing a large standard, on which was represented the infant Jesus with his holy mother. All the algonquins—and especially the christians, who had been invited to assist in the pious function—followed, and accompanied the infant Jesus. They marched, then, in that order toward the village, Chanting the litanies of the virgin, and went into a Cabin of our hurons, where they had prepared for Jesus a lodging, as appropriate as they could make it. There they offered thanksgivings and prayers, in accordance with their devotion; and the divine child was conducted back to the church and replaced in the grotto. The Christian algonquins were afterward invited by the Christian hurons to a feast . . .

After this feast, at which, according to their Custom, the hurons did not eat, another and a special one was prepared for all the Christian and non-Christian hurons, spread by the officers in turn. This feast was preceded by a dance, as is their custom, whose sole object was that they might Rejoice together at the favor that they had received in the Visit which the new-born child had paid to their village. This dance is performed by the women only, as I said,—ranging themselves in two parallel lines at the two Sides of a Cabin, having in their hands a kind of Castanet. Those who are officers commence the Song and dance; they have some words to which they apply one of their airs, and these form the refrain of their Song which every one is to repeat to the same air. While the One who has Begun Goes on with her Song agreeably to the words which have served her for a refrain,— very often, however, varying the air,—she Runs and bustles about between these two ranks in a singular manner. In this there is nothing, as formerly, to violate decency, especially on occasions in which

they claim to honor God. Meanwhile the others—repeating at certain intervals the words which form the refrain, and which explain the intention of the one who is dancing—sound their Castanets, and move sometimes one foot, sometimes the other, to Certain measures without leaving their places. When some word which pleases them occurs in the Song they redouble the noise of their castanets.

OUR JOYFUL'ST FEAST

A former captain in the army of Cromwell, George Wither (1588-1667) might have been expected to disapprove of Christmas. Yet his "A Christmas Carol" is far from Puritanical.

So now is come our joyful'st feast;
Let every man be jolly.
Each room with ivy-leaves is dressed,
And every post with holly.
   Though some churls at our mirth repine
   Round your foreheads garlands twine,
   Drown sorrow in a cup of wine,
And let us all be merry.

Now all our neighbours' chimneys smoke,
And Christmas blocks are burning;
The ovens they with baked meats choke,
And all their spits are turning.
   Without the door let sorrow lie,
   And if for cold it hap to die,
   We'll bury 't in a Christmas pie,
And everymore be merry.

Now every lad is wondrous trim,
And no man minds his labour;
Our lasses have provided them
A bag-pipe and a tabor.
   Young men, and maids, and girls and boys,

Give life to one another's joys,
  And you anon shall by their noise
Perceive that they are merry.

Rank misers now do sparing shun,
Their hall of music soundeth,
And dogs thence with whole shoulders run,
So all things there aboundeth.
  The country-folk themselves advance,
  For crowdy-mutton's come out of France;
  And Jack shall pipe, and Jill shall dance,
And all the town be merry. . . .

The wenches with their wassail bowls
About the streets are singing,

The boys are come to catch the owls,
The wild mare in is bringing.
  Our kitchen-boy hath broke his box,
  And to the dealing of the ox
  Our honest neighbours come by flocks,
And here they will be merry. . . .

Then wherefore in these merry days
Should we, I pray, be duller?
No; let us sing our roundelays
To make our mirth the fuller.
  And, whilst thus inspired we sing,
  Let all the streets with echoes ring;
  Woods, and hills, and everything,
Bear witness we are merry.

𝕳uron 𝕴ndian 𝕮arol

This Christmas carol, "Jesous Ahatonnia" ("Jesus Is Born"), was written for the Huron Indians in the Huron tongue by Father Jean de Brébeuf. Like the missionaries among the European pagans, he described the Nativity to the tribes in terms of their customs.

'Twas in the moon of win-ter time When all the birds had fled,
That migh-ty Git-chi Man-i-tou sent an-gel choirs in-stead;
Be-fore their light the stars grew dim, And wond'ring hun-ters heard the hymn:
Je-sus your King is born, Je-sus is born! In ex-cel-sis glo-ri-a!

V

MANOR HOUSE HOLIDAY

HE AFTERWARDS FELL INTO AN account of the diversions which had passed in his house during the holidays, for Sir Roger, after the laudable custom of his ancestors, always keeps open house at Christmas. I learned from him that he had killed eight fat hogs for this season, that he had dealt about his chines very liberally amongst his neighbours, and that in particular he had sent a string of hogs' puddings with a pack of Cards to every poor family in the Parish. "I have often thought," says Sir Roger, "it happens very well that Christmas should fall out in the middle of the winter. It is the most dead, uncomfortable time of the year, when the poor people would suffer very much from their poverty and cold, if they had not good cheer, warm fires, and Christmas gambols to support them." "ESSAYS OF JOSEPH ADDISON"

POLITE SOCIETY *plays cards in a Hogarth painting. Card games and informality were the new Christmas mode in the 18th Century.*

A FREER,
MORE
SOCIAL
CELEBRATION

A NOBLE OTHELLO *gestures on an Italian puppet stage. Marionette shows were at the peak of their vogue in the 18th Century.*

THE AUSTERE YEARS of the Puritan Commonwealth ended in 1660, and Christmas returned to England with the restoration of Catholic King Charles II. And like the monarchy, Christmas came back shorn of some of its old cavalier flamboyance. Its festivities became more social than ceremonial, more middle-class than regal. Its chief celebrants were no longer kings and nobles but the country squire and the rich merchant. No more aristocratic feasts of boar were carried in to the songs of minstrels or carolers, but a side of beef was served, or a pig, or turkey.

Besides this new informality, new humanitarian impulses entered the gentry's celebration of Christmas. An almanac of 1723, describing one squire's Christmas, remarked that he "invites his Tenants and Labourers, and with a good Sirloin of Roast Beef, and a few pitchers of nappy ale or beer, he wisheth them all a merry Christmas." After the meal, there would be dancing and songs, and often the night would end with ghost stories being told by the fire.

The squire often remembered the poor. One man's will in 1729 provided that each Christmas 20 pieces of beef should be doled out to those "such as had no relief on that day."

In the cities, the great masques of a previous age and the great silence of Puritan times were replaced by new forms of old public entertainment—the pantomime and the puppet play. John Rich, a London theater manager, introduced the Christmas pantomime to England in 1717, and his fantastic productions—with their Harlequins, Columbines, giants, fairies, fiends and dizzying plots—were a tremendous success. The puppet shows of the time were equally lavish. One, "Mr. Pinkethman's Pantheon," advertised fully 100 puppets and a show that "deserves to be esteemed the greatest wonder of the age."

Yet even more popular than such extravaganzas was card playing. No 18th Century Christmas was complete without it. Every squire got down his pack and every city party had its social game of whist or piquet. There were other games too, even less formal, that were played with gusto upstairs by the host and guests, and belowstairs by the servants: Blindman's Buff, Hot Cockles, Hunt the Slipper.

This genteel and social celebration survived, in America, among the Southern aristocracy. The country's first Christmas had been a Southern one when, in 1607, the Jamestown settlers had feasted and rejoiced in cavalier fashion. George Washington carried on this tradition. His Twelfth Night festivities of 1759, doubled in joy by his marriage that day to Martha Custis, were truly exuberant. A yule log blazed, firecrackers exploded, the halls were hung with green, and the party sat down to a generous feast. For Christmas, 1760—and for Christmases thereafter until the war —Washington, his bride and two stepchildren spent similarly gay holidays at Mount Vernon.

But America's Christmases were as varied as the peoples who had come to the new land. In general, Catholics, Episcopalians, Lutherans and the Dutch settlers rejoiced both in church and out, while Baptists, Presbyterians and Quakers tended to shun all observance of the holiday. In New England, an Irishman was chased out of town in 1755 when people discovered he was "a Christmas Man," but in Pennsylvania, one dour preacher noted, "Christmas & New Year holly days are seasons of wild mirth & disorder." In New York on December 5, the Dutch welcomed St. Nicholas, who visited homes and gave presents to the good and switches to the bad. In Missouri and Louisiana, French children put out their shoes for *le petit Noël* to fill, and in the Spanish Southwest, Mary and Joseph's long search for an inn was re-enacted.

Revolution, which strengthened the ties among America's many peoples, did not destroy their variety. Nor did America, in its revolt, utterly reject the traditions of its parent nation, England. It kept as much graciousness as it could afford, but felt no longer obliged to follow the fashions of any court. But the French, in their revolt, tried to destroy Christmas along with their monarchy. Church bells were melted for their bronze, worship was suspended on Christmas Day, and the *gâteau des rois,* or cake of the Kings, was renamed "the cake of Equality." By 1830, democracy had taken root in much of Europe, as it had in America, and the new Christmas was a democratic and all-inclusive one.

A CHRISTMAS PUPPET PLAY *in Venice is performed by figures a foot high. They include (from left to right) Brighella, Pantaloon, Harlequin, Columbine, The Lover and The Lady. Puppets were as popular in England during the Christmas season as they were in Italy. A London churchman complained that the puppet shows were packed but "we have a very thin house."*

ST. NICHOLAS' SINISTER HELPER, *Knecht Ruprecht, frightens children who do not know their prayers. He was also known as Black Peter.*

HOPES AND FEARS FROM THE PAGAN PAST

The Christmas season retained traces of old pagan fears as late as the 18th Century. To the superstitious the shift from the old year to the new was menacing—a time when good and evil hung in the balance. Knecht Ruprecht, the assistant to St. Nicholas shown in the German print above, was as capable of punishing as he was of rewarding, and the horns on his head reveal his demonic origin. Even St. Lucy, the patron saint of light, had her darker side; in the imagination of some Germanic folk she became the *Lutzelfrau*, a fearsome witch who rode the winds at Yuletide and who had to be bribed with little gifts. Perchta was another German Christmas witch. In south Germany, masked children, carrying brooms, went from house to house begging presents in her name. In other parts of Europe, the star-singers—a Dutch group is shown at the right in an 18th Century painting—roamed through the cities. They were welcomed for their songs and also for the blessing they were thought to give the house they stopped at. If they drew three crosses on a house, and the initials of the Kings, it was thought no harm would visit there.

STAR-SINGERS, *children dressed as the Three Kings and carrying star-shaped paper lanterns, sing carols to a family on Twelfth Night, while one boy reaches out for a gift. These costumed Christmas singers, once common throughout Europe, went from door to door, presenting pageants.*

Oh, I wish that coach were mine.

Let me look at that knife.

Here's money for that pair of pliers.

I would like some of those blocks.

What is it, boy? Just tell me.

Now then, what do you want?

I wanted a smaller lamp.

I have some splendid things, madam.

What do you want, little mouse?

I'd like an angel like that one.

Yes, that's the wagon I want.

These marbles are what I'd really like.

A FEAST OF LOVE *is observed by Moravians, a Germanic Protestant sect, with a simple meal of buns and coffee. This American print points out the* pastor (A), *the boys (B) and girls (C), and the servers (D and E). Moravian settlers celebrated the love feast in the U.S. as early as 1753.*

A TIME OF
ABUNDANCE
AND
SHARING

By the 18th Century, the great Christmas fair in Nuremberg, Germany, was centuries old. But it still began, as in earliest days, in the first week of December, and at its opening a child dressed as an angel welcomed visitors. Hundreds of booths filled the square. Among their wares were the seasonal *Lebkuchen,* or ginger

cake, as well as figurines of the infant Jesus. These were given as presents, continuing the Nurembergers' medieval tradition of "giving away the Christ child."

This affectionate generosity was also basic to the love feast which Moravians celebrated with Scripture, food and music. The Moravians, an

early sect of Germanic Protestants, migrated to America in the 18th Century. Their love feasts continued in their new homeland, and so did their gifts of love. On Christmas 1760, it is recorded, Moravians in Bethabara, North Carolina, brought to their English neighbors a "pretty Christmas verse and a gingercake."

AN ARRAY OF BOOTHS *is open at the old Nuremberg Christmas market. The 12 shown in these German prints (opposite) display a variety of wares ranging from wooden angels to oil lanterns.*

High Life below Stairs.

A GAY SWIRL OF SERVANTS *celebrates Christmas in a room decked with holly and mistletoe. In this satiric English print by Robert Cruikshank, a three-man band (left) provides music for dancing, flirting or, as in the case of the man at far right, simply collapsing at three in the morning.*

NEW JOYS AND FREEDOMS

The democratic spirit, vigorous in America and in Europe in the late 18th Century, brought with it new attitudes toward the celebration of Christmas as well as a new freedom for all classes *(above)*. The opulent entertainments of the courts became increasingly discreet, and the organized anarchy devised by Lords of Misrule for the upper classes dwindled to parlor games. In America, the mummers' shows reflected the chang-ing times: the old battle between St. George and the Dragon was being presented as a fight between George Washington and Oliver Cromwell.

In England, pantomime arrived on the stage. Actors in the legitimate theater looked down on this vastly popular entertainment. The satirical poet Alexander Pope scorned panto-mime as a coarse show that "Dull-ness and her sons admire," and he described its usual plot as: "A fire, a jig, a battle, and a ball, / Till one wide conflagration swallows all."

The new spectacles, numerous and popular as they were, formed but a small part of the typical Christmas. In the city a man's home, rather than the theater or the court, was now the main scene of celebration. And in the country the squire cele-brated with decorum, offering food, drinks for all, a dance—and even a visit to church on Christmas Day.

A NEW CAST OF CHARACTERS *for a Twelfth Night pantomime is presented in this chart of punning riddles. These fantasies were the most popular stage events of the English Christmas.*

Park's New Twelfth-Night Characters.

KING OF HEARTS.   QUEEN OF HEARTS.   DICKY DAGGERWOOD.   MRS. DAGGERANDO.   LORD BANDASH.   LADY BOW-WELL.

1. When is a king not a king?
2. Why does her Majesty resemble St. Swithin?
3. Why is a melancholy young lady the pleasantest of all companions?
4. What description of drinking glass is more droll than others?
5. Why should a thin man make a better barge than a fat man?
6. If a single burner be taken from a chandelier, why should it be brighter?

SIR BENJAMIN BOUNCE.   COUNTESS FLY AWAY.   SWELLERANDO.   LADY LOW SLEEVE.   LORD DUMBLE DUM DEARY.   LADY LOVEWELL.

7. Why are the first rays of the morning like an infuriated bull?
8. Why is being cheated like a cockney lover's parting word?
9. Why is a man who beats his wife like a drunkard?
10. Why is a sick young lady like anything thrown from the hand?
11. Why is the chariot of Venus like the discoverer of the last planet?
12. Why are lover's sighs like long stockings?

LORD FLIRT AWAY.   LADY RAMBLE.   SAMUEL SPRUCE.   LADY LANGUISH.   SPANTU LONG TONG SONG.   SING LING TING.

13. Why is a statue like a fig?
14. Why is a little demon sitting on a pent-house like a poor man?
15. When is leather like rust?
16. Why are comic songs like gross blunders?
17. When is a blacksmith a hermit?
18. Why is 4s. 9d. a week, a government allowance?

LORD LOLLYPOP.   MRS. STRUT.   SIR CHARLES C-GAR-UM.   LADY WARBLE.   DAVID BANDASH.   MADAME MANDOLINE.

19. Why is a wife like a joint of pork?
20. When is a sailor above his commander?
21. Why does a carpenter live on addition?
22. Why is a monkey like an artist?
23. When is Lent not Lent?
24. Why is a baker like a grave digger?

LADY DASHALL.   LORD DASHAWAY.   GEORGIE GALLOPPARA.   FANNY FANDANGO.

25. Why does a printer dislike pastry?
26. Why is an unbound book like a young maiden in bed?
27. Why is a coxcomb like a law volume?
28. Why are butchers the strongest men in creation.

KEY TO THE CONUNDRUMS.

1. When he is a king-dumb (kingdom)
2. Because she always reigns.
3. Because she is always a-musing.
4. That which is called a rummer.
5. Because he's lighter.
6. Because its lighter by a lamp.
7. Because its a-roarer (aurora).
8. Because its a-do (adieu.)
9. Because he's addicted to lick-her. (liquor).
10. Because it is a missile (miss-ill)
11. Because it's her shell (Herschel).
12. Because they are weigh-ohs! (high-lows).
13. Because it is an FIG (effigy).
14. Because he is an imp-over-a-shed (impoverished).
15. When it is ox-hide (oxide).
16. Because they are absurd ditties. (absurdities)
17. When he is an anchor-wright. (anchorite)
18. Because its under the crown.
19. Because she's a spare rib.
20. When he's mastheaded.
21. Because he lives by the odze.
22. Because he imitates nature.
23. When it is religiously kept.
24. Because he deals in dead men.
25. Because he is not fond of pye.
26. Because she's done up in sheets.
27. Because he's bound in calf.
28. Because they have more joints.

Printed and Published by A. Park, No. 47, Leonard Street, Finsbury.

THE SQUIRE'S BANQUET

"The Sketch Book of Geoffrey Crayon, Gent." by Washington Irving (1783-1859) presents a classic description of Christmas in the English manor house tradition. In this excerpt from the book, the squire's Christmas dinner is bountiful but the aristocratic fare of earlier times is absent. A pig's head and pheasant pie replace the traditional boar's head and peacock pie.

The dinner was served up in the great hall, where the squire always held his Christmas banquet. A blazing crackling fire of logs had been heaped on to warm the spacious apartment, and the flame went sparkling and wreathing up the wide-mouthed chimney. . . .

We were ushered into this banquetting scene with the sound of minstrelsy; the old harper being seated on a stool beside the fireplace, and twanging the roast beef of old England, with a vast deal more power than melody. Never did Christmas board display a more goodly and gracious assemblage of countenances; those who were not handsome were, at least, happy; and happiness is a rare improver of your hard-favoured visage. The parson said grace, which was not a short familiar one, such as is commonly addressed to the deity, in these unceremonious days; but a long, courtly, well-worded one, of the ancient school. There was now a pause, as if something was expected, when suddenly the Butler entered the hall, with some degree of bustle; he was attended by a servant on each side with a large wax light, and bore a silver dish, on which was an enormous pig's head, decorated with rosemary, with a lemon in its mouth, which was placed with great formality at the head of the table. The moment this pageant made its appearance, the harper struck up a flourish; at the conclusion of which the young Oxonian, on receiving a hint from the squire, gave, with an air of the most comic gravity, an old carol, the first verse of which was as follows:

> *Caput apri defero*
> *Reddens laudes Domino.*
> The boar's head in hand bring I,
> With garlands gay and rosemary.
> I pray you all synge merily,
> *Qui estis in convivio . . .*

When the cloth was removed, the butler brought in a huge silver vessel of rare and curious workmanship, which he placed before the squire. Its appearance was hailed with acclamation; being the Wassail Bowl, so renowned in Christmas festivity. The contents had been prepared by the squire himself, being a beverage on the skilful mixture of which he particularly prided himself; alleging that it was too abstruse and complex for the comprehension of an ordinary servant. It was a potation, indeed, that might well make the heart of a toper leap within him; consisting of the richest and raciest wines, highly spiced and sweetened, with roasted apples bobbing about the surface.

The old gentleman's whole countenance beamed with a serene look of in-dwelling delight, as he stirred this mighty bowl. Having raised it to his lips, with a hearty wish of a merry Christmas to all present, he sent it brimming round the board, for every one to follow his example according to the primitive custom; pronouncing it "the ancient fountain of good fellowship, where all hearts met together." . . .

After the dinner table was removed, the hall was given up to the younger members of the family, who, prompted to all kind of noisy mirth by the Oxonian and Master Simon, made its old walls ring with their merriment, as they played at romping games. I delight in witnessing the gambols of children, and particularly at this happy holiday-season, and could not help stealing out of the drawing room on hearing one of their peals of laughter. . . .

The door suddenly flew open, and a whimsical train came trooping into the room, that might almost have been mistaken for the breaking up of the court of Fairy. That indefatigable spirit, Master Simon, in the faithful discharge of his duties as lord of misrule, had conceived the idea of a Christmas mummery, or masqueing; and having called in to his assistance the Oxonian and the young officer, who were equally ripe for any thing that should occasion romping and merriment, they had carried it into instant effect. The old housekeeper had been consulted; the antique clothes presses and wardrobes rummaged and made to yield up the reliques of finery that had not seen the light for several generations; the younger part of the company had been privately convened from the parlour and hall, and the whole had been bedizened out, into a burlesque imitation of an antique masque.

Master Simon led the van as "ancient Christmas," quaintly apparel'd in short cloak and ruff, and a hat that might have served for a village steeple, from under which, his nose curved boldly forth, with a frost bitten bloom that seemed the very trophy of a December blast. He was accompanied by the blue eyed romp, dished up as "Dame mince pie," in the venerable magnificence of faded brocade, long stomacher, peaked hat, and high heeled shoes. The young officer figured in genuine Kendal Green as Robin Hood; the fair Julia in a pretty rustic dress as Maid Marian. The rest of the train had been metamorphosed in various ways; the girls trussed up in the finery of their great grandmothers, and the striplings bewhiskered with burnt cork, and fantastically arrayed to support the characters of Roast Beef, Plum Porridge, and other worthies celebrated in ancient masqueings. The whole was under the control of the Oxonian, in the appropriate character of Misrule . . .

It was inspiring to see wild-eyed frolick and warm-hearted hospitality breaking out from among the chills and glooms of winter, and old age throwing off its apathy, and catching once more the freshness of youthful enjoyment. I felt

an interest in the scene, also, from the consideration that these fleeting customs were posting fast into oblivion; and that this was, perhaps, the only family in England in which the whole of them were still punctiliously observed. There was a quaintness, too, mingled with all this revelry, that gave it a peculiar zest: it was suited to the time and place; and as the old manor house almost reeled with mirth and wassail, it seemed echoing back the joviality of long-departed years.

Dreams of Grandeur

At Christmas Eve of 1811, Napoleon had Europe at his mercy. His military power is contrasted with the gentle spirit of the holiday in this fanciful scene from "Imperial Christmas."

It is Christmas eve of the year 1811, and Napoleon has been working alone in his office at the palace of the Tuileries since 10 o'clock in the evening. The large room is almost entirely dark. Here and there, in the shadow, shine some gilded objects, such as the frame of a picture, the heads of lions adorning the arms of a chair, and the heavy tassel of a curtain. Under their shades of metal, the wax candles of the two candelabra light only the large table incumbered with atlases and thick books bound in green morocco and stamped with the "N" and the crown.

The master has been working for nearly two hours, and on the geographical maps and on the charts marking the situation of his armies he bends his formidable forehead—that forehead heavy with thoughts, heavy as the world of which he meditates the conquest.

He has already the greatness of Cæsar and Charlemagne; he also wishes that of Alexander. He dreams this dream without wondering at it. He knows already the Orient; he has left behind him there an immortal legend. The Nile saw him one day, a thin general with long hair, mounted on a dromedary. On the banks of the Ganges the heavy Emperor, in his gray redingote, will need the elephant of Porus. He knows how to lead the people and how to fanaticize them. He will command soldiers over there with bronze faces, wearing turbans of white muslin; he will see mixed with his staff rajahs sparkling with jewels, and he will consult the monstrous idols, raising their 10 arms above their mitre of diamonds, about his destiny; since not long ago, in Egypt, the flat-nosed Sphinx, before which he dreamed, leaning on his saber, would not betray its secret. . .

But suddenly he raises his head with a movement of surprise. In his office, tightly closed and of which the heavy curtains are lowered, whence comes that strange and profound murmur? It seems as if the large gold bees embroidered on the silk hangings all begin to hum. The Emperor listens more attentively, and in that noise he distinguishes vibrations of brass.

"Ah! yes—Christmas—the midnight mass.". . .

The Emperor dreams—and in the confused sound of the bells which call to the midnight Mass he imagines he hears the cadenced march of the troops and the rolling of the ammunition wagons far away on the icy roads of Germany and Poland. Intoxicated with paternal ambition, he thinks more than ever of the Grand Army and of the conquest of Russia and India, and he swears to himself to leave to his heir all the thrones of the Old World. He has already given to him the city of St. Peter for a toy; the new-born will soon have other holy cities among his playthings. . .

And while the Emperor pursues his monstrous chimera, imagining the reign of his son and of his son's successors on the entire world, and fancying himself, Napoleon, having become, in the course of time and of legend, a fabulous myth, a new Mars, a solar god triumphant in the midst of the Zodiac of his 12 marshals, the bells still ring, joyously, triumphantly, desperately, in honor of the poor little Child born at Bethlehem, who really conquered the world 1,900 years ago, not with blood and with victories, but with the word of peace and of love, and who shall reign over souls in the endless chain of centuries.

CHRISTMAS WITH LEWIS AND CLARK

Two Christmases in the wilderness, in 1804 and 1805, are described by explorers Meriwether Lewis and William Clark in journal entries.

Tuesday, 25th December 1804. We were awakened before day by a discharge of three platoons from the party. We had told the Indians not to visit us as it was one of our great medicine days, so that the men remained at home and amused themselves various ways, particularly with dancing, in which they take great pleasure. The American flag was hoisted for the first time in the fort; the best provisions we had were brought out, and this, with a little brandy, enabled them to pass the day in great festivity. Wednesday, 25th December 1805. We were awakened at daylight by a discharge of firearms, which was followed by a song from the men, as a compliment to us on the return of Christmas, which we have always been accustomed to observe as a day of rejoicing. After breakfast we divided our remaining stock of tobacco, which amounted to twelve carrots, into two parts; one of which we distributed among such of the party as made use of it; making a present of a handkerchief to the others. The remainder of the day was passed in good spirits, though there was nothing in our situation to excite much gayety.

A GOOD GAME OF WHIST
♣ ♦ ♠ ♥

As Christmas became more domestic, cards became increasingly popular as a holiday diversion. Here is a portrait of a dedicated whist player, from an essay by Charles Lamb (1775-1834).

"A clear fire, a clean hearth, and the rigour of the game." This was the celebrated *wish* of old Sarah Battle (now with God), who, next to her devotions, loved a good game of whist. She was none of your lukewarm gamesters, your half-and-half players, who have no objection to take a hand, if you want one to make up a rubber; who affirm that they have no pleasure in winning; that they like to win one game and lose another; that they can while away an hour very agreeably at a card-table, but are indifferent whether they play or no; and will desire an adversary, who has slipped a wrong card, to take it up and play another. These insufferable triflers are the curse of a table. One of these flies will spoil a whole pot. Of such it may be said that they do not play at cards, but only play at playing at them.

Sarah Battle was none of that breed. She detested them, as I do, from her heart and soul, and would not, save upon a striking emergency, willingly seat herself at the same table with them. She loved a thorough-paced partner, a determined enemy. She took, and gave, no concessions. She hated favours. She never made a revoke, nor ever passed it over in her adversary without exacting the utmost forfeiture. She fought a good fight: cut and thrust. She held not her good sword (her cards) "like a dancer." She sate bolt upright; and neither showed you her cards, nor desired to see yours. All people have their blind side—their superstitions; and I have heard her declare, under the rose, that hearts was her favourite suit . . .

Quadrille, she has often told me, was her first love; but whist had engaged her maturer esteem. The former, she said, was showy and specious, and likely to allure young persons. The uncertainty and quick shifting of partners—a thing which the constancy of whist abhors; the dazzling supremacy and regal investiture of Spadille—absurd, as she justly observed, in the pure aristocracy of whist, where his crown and garter gave him no proper power above his brother-nobility of the Aces;—the giddy vanity, so taking to the inexperienced, of playing alone; above all, the overpowering attractions of a *Sans Prendre Vole,*—to the triumph of which there is certainly nothing parallel or approaching, in the contingencies of whist;—all these, she would say, make quadrille a game of captivation to the young and enthusiastic. But whist was the *solider* game: that was her word. It was a long meal; not, like quadrille, a feast of snatches . . .

Masters in This Hall

The verses of this Christmas carol were composed by the English poet William Morris around 1860. Its music, a traditional French air, embodies the vigorous rhythms of 15th Century carols sung in colorful processions to church.

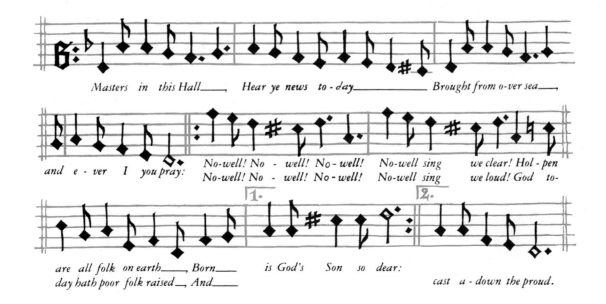

VI
THE VICTORIAN CHRISTMAS

THE CHRISTMAS TREE IS ANNUALLY prepared by her Majesty's command for the Royal children. . . . The tree employed for this festive purpose is a young fir of about eight feet high, and has six tiers of branches. On each tier, or branch, are arranged a dozen wax tapers. Pendant from the branches are elegant trays, baskets, *bonbonnières,* and other receptacles for sweetmeats of the most varied and expensive kind; and of all forms, colours, and degrees of beauty. Fancy cakes, gilt gingerbread and eggs filled with sweetmeats, are also suspended by variously-coloured ribbons from the branches. The tree, which stands upon a table covered with white damask, is supported at the root by piles of sweets of a larger kind, and by toys and dolls of all descriptions, suited to the youthful fancy. . . . On the summit of the tree stands the small figure of an angel, with outstretched wings, holding in each hand a wreath. "THE ILLUSTRATED LONDON NEWS," 1848

A TIMEWORN MEMENTO, *this elaborate Christmas card dates from Victoria's happy reign, when the greeting cards first appeared.*

FINALLY, CHRISTMAS REACHES OUT TO ALL HOMES

A VICTORIAN TIPPLER *sniffs his Christmas wine with delight. Many 19th Century recipes mixed wine and ale in wassail bowls.*

CHRISTMAS exuded middle-class cheer in the age of Victoria, the 64 years (1837-1901) in which the rotund little queen presided over the British Empire and the British Empire more or less presided over the world. In urban areas of America and Europe as well as in England, December stirred up a great hustle and bustle of ordinary folk to prepare for a more bountiful holiday. Improved roads and rails carried increasing numbers of people home for Christmas. Stores sold an ever-greater volume and variety of goods at Christmas. With the start of England's penny post in 1839, Christmas cards appeared; fancy and colorful, they soon spread across two continents, adding their cheerful bit to the general air of holiday well-being. Kindly, content and optimistic, Victorians recast the traditional figure of Father Christmas in their own image, transforming St. Nicholas, the formidable judge of childrens' behavior, into the merry, open-handed gift-giver called Santa Claus.

The queen, who heartily endorsed this more prosperous Christmas, much resembled its chief beneficiaries. Victoria, said a faithful historian of her time, "was possessed in high degree of queenly instincts and dignity, but they were softened and popularized by a mind and emotional nature of great simplicity. In herself she was not very different from her female subjects in humble stations of life."

Victoria's own Christmases typified the middle-class celebration of the holiday. The queen loved her hearth and children; she and her husband, the German Prince Albert of Saxe-Coburg, seldom left home for public festivities. She loved her candlelit Christmas trees with their gingerbread decorations, and she was proud that Albert had done so much to make the German tree custom an institution in England. And the royal couple, like their people, were unabashedly sentimental, especially during the holidays. On one occasion, they were transfixed by a flourish of midnight trumpets announcing the start of the New Year. That music, Victoria wrote in her journal, "quite affected dear Albert, who turned pale and had tears in his eyes and pressed my hand very warmly. It touched me, for I felt he must be thinking of his dear native country which he left for me."

To a woman of such feeling, charity was second nature. As one Victorian noted, "Her Majesty's Royal bounties to the poor . . . are well known, the ancient Christmas and New Year's gifts being dispensed with great generosity. . . . Then there is the distribution of the beef, a most interesting feature of the Royal Bounty."

The widespread need for alms was but one sign that the new industrial prosperity had not reached large segments of society. Even on Christmas, countless poor wretches, including children, worked long hours in the mines and factories. Never did their slum homes seem grimmer to them than on Christmas Day. And never were protests in their behalf more vociferous than at Christmas. One of the most eloquent spokesmen for humanitarian reform was the novelist Charles Dickens. His story, "A Christmas Carol," wrung honest tears from worldly intellectuals as well as greengrocers' wives. Slowly, reforms were adopted. One of these, incorporated in the Bank Holiday Act of 1871, made Christmas an official day of rest in England, and 19 years later America's last laggard, the territory of Oklahoma, followed suit.

By then, Victoria's long reign was drawing to its end. The middle-class home Christmas that emerged in her age has changed little since, except to grow even more inclusive. Yet the increased pace of life in the 20th Century fills many moderns with nostalgia for that earlier age—that warm, safe, contented time when there was leisure enough to enjoy Christmas to the full. For them, the thought of Christmas still conjures up a host of images that are distinctly Victorian: of huge family gatherings in thatch-roofed country cottages; of trim coaches and horse-drawn sleighs; of men in stovepipe hats, prim women whose skirts brush the snows, children in long, bright mufflers. These quaint scenes still adorn modern Christmas cards. And so do sentimental pictures of the "waits," those Victorian carolers who wandered the streets in small groups, ready to sing for a few pennies. In London many of them were young Cockneys, and when they burst into song their accents rang out clear:

'Ark, the 'erald h'angels sing,
Glory to the newborn King.

PLUMP MOLLY DUMPLING, *the epitome of the Victorian cook, plunges her Christmas pudding into water. After cooking, this delectable fruity mass was doused with brandy and served aflame.*

THE FINAL HALF-HOUR *before Christmas dinner is gently satirized in this Victorian print. Though grandpa snoozes, the atmosphere is tense. The children ar*

BRAVE FAMILIES AT THEIR FEASTING

English Victorians, looking back on Christmas banquets of the past, considered their holiday dinner quite restrained. But in setting a table to match their rising standard of living, they consumed enough to make their descendants blanch. The serious eating on Christmas Day began about 1 p.m. The typical lunch included soup, stuffed turkey, plum pudding and mince pie. Then came an elaborate tea at 5 o'clock.

The principal meal of the day—it is drolly depicted in the Victorian prints on these pages—began around 9. There was trout, a suckling pig roasted whole on the spit, candy and cake, and several kinds of wine. It

IN A FLURRY OF TOASTS, *the Christmas dinner draws to a close with mince pies and plum pudding on the table. Even baby has been brought down to share the excitement.*

...restless, and relations with the help are probably strained.

took courage to face up to such a feast, and satirists like William Makepeace Thackeray chortled with glee over the disappointing dishes and the big food bills that inevitably ensued. But most Victorians enjoyed every minute and every morsel of it, and they worked off their postprandial lethargy in gay romps and games.

AFTER THE DINNER, *the young people whirl to music by their elders, while the children valiantly continue to gorge themselves and stuff their dog with the last of the goodies.*

IGNITING THE YULE LOG *in a kitchen oven, the patriarch of a French family chants, "May our Lord fill us with happiness. And if next year we have not more, O God, let us not have less."*

LIGHTS FOR EUROPE'S MYRIAD CELEBRATIONS

In Western Europe in the 19th Century, the Christmas season glowed with light in celebrations that were much the same as they are today. In Spain, children carrying lamps on poles scattered through city streets to light the way for the Three Kings bearing gifts. In Italy, candles were lit at ornate crèches in churches, town squares and in fine homes draped with lemon blossoms and periwinkles. In German homes, the halls were purposefully kept dark so that the children would be dazzled as they burst into brilliantly lit rooms where candles burned on the Christmas trees *(opposite)* and presents awaited. In Sweden, lovely young girls risked singeing their hair to honor their parents *(below)*. In France, where the *bûche de Noël* (yule log) was ceremoniously ignited *(above)*, every window on Paris' great boulevards blazed with light on Christmas night and, one English visitor noted, "even the table of the poor chestnut vendor has an additional lamp." Similar customs, as well as many unique ones, had also reached their present form in Eastern Europe *(next pages)*.

A GERMAN CHRISTMAS ROOM *is a candlelit paradise. Besides toys each child received a "Bunte Teller," or plate of sweets.*

LIGHTING THE DARK, *a Swedish girl appears before her parents wearing a white dress and a bonnet of candles. She brings them music and coffee at 2 a.m. on December 13, St. Lucia's day.*

AN ARISTOCRATIC FAMILY *in 19th Century Russia examines presents around the Christmas trees. In 20th Century Russia, as in 17th Century Englan*

OLD WAYS IN EASTERN EUROPE

A pre-Christmas fast, widely and diversely observed today, had become a vital part of the holiday in Eastern Europe by the 19th Century. In Russia, no meat was served for 40 days, and on the day before Christmas, there was no food at all until the first evening star appeared. Then,

after Mass, Russians went home to feast on foods bought from peasants in open sleighs—pastrami, pigs and geese, duck and quail.

Christmas trees by the thousands went on sale in Moscow three days before the great day. Decorations for the trees and for the house were

Christmas was banned for a time and then restored.

A GOOD-LUCK CAKE *is blessed by a Serbian family, whose members cluster around it holding lighted candles. Hidden in the cake is a silver coin, said to bring good fortune to the finder.*

A BLINDFOLDED GOOSE, *turned loose at a German Christmas party, is urged on toward the oldest unmarried girl. According to legend, the girl whom the bird touches first will wed first.*

so expensive that most were home-made. Apples and tangerines were strung up, and dolls were made of dried fruit and candy. Walnuts were dipped in egg white, rolled in sheets of gold foil and hung by threads.

Old social customs and folk super-stitions added charm to the festivi-ties. On the third or fourth day of Christmas, Russian servants in aris-tocratic homes renewed their annu-al contracts with their employers or looked for new positions. In either case, the negotiations called for sev-eral drinks. Meanwhile, little work was done for reasons explained by many old sayings. It was also the season for fortunetelling, for seeing auguries of the future everywhere. To many Russians, a frosty Christ-mas meant a rich grain harvest next year. Starry skies promised a good crop of peas, but if the skies stayed dark, the cows would be productive.

HAPPY TRAPPERS *for the Hudson's Bay Company greet Christmas beside a roaring fire. As the others sing, one woodsman proposes a toast from his dog sled.*

NOSTALGIC COWBOYS *are shown at their revels in the 1891 Christmas issue of "Frank Leslie's" magazine. "Leslie's" entitled the picture, "Sweet, Sweet Home."*

THE HOLIDAY OUT WEST

Christmas in the American West inspired many fanciful pictures by popular artists in their city studios. But if frontier celebrations seldom included a pudding *(above)*, they were often as sentimental as the artists' versions of them. Christmas sharp-

WELL-EQUIPPED HUNTERS *prepare a Christmas pudding in their wilderness camp. The deer hanging in the background probably provided suet, the main ingredient in the dessert. But few frontier hunters took to the woods with the rich fruits and spices required for a proper pudding.*

ened the yearning of pioneer families separated from old friends. In gold camps and cow towns, lonely men banged tin pans, fired their pistols, sang noisily and held all-male dances. One of three miners who spent a Christmas in camp recalled,

"I took out of my belt two heavy nuggets . . . and gave one to each of them. It was a poor enough gift. Gold was a common commodity with us. They'd have appreciated a hot biscuit a lot more."

But the West had its traditional Christmases long before the country was fully settled. One German visitor to Texas in 1846 reported seeing "a richly decorated and illuminated Christmas tree . . . where . . . scarcely two years ago the camp fires of the wild Comanches were burning."

A LONG WINTER'S NAP

ON, DONDER AND BLITZEN

DOWN THE CHIMNEY

STRAIGHT TO HIS WORK

AN EARLY SANTA CLAUS, *seen in 1849 sketches for Moore's "A Visit from St. Nicholas," shows less bulk and cheer than the elf in the poem.*

A NEW LOOK FOR SANTA CLAUS

At the start of the 19th Century, the traditional Christmastime gift-giver was St. Nicholas, a tall, stern patriarch in bishop's robes. By the end of the century he was Santa Claus, a tubby, jovial figure in a red suit. This remarkable transformation was helped along by several writers: they gave St. Nicholas a pipe, a prosperous air, a single reindeer. But the biggest contributions were made by two of the unlikeliest men—a serious classical scholar and a famous political cartoonist.

Clement C. Moore was a professor at an Episcopal seminary in New York. He was opposed to "frivolous amusements," yet to please his children he devoted a few hours to frivolous versifying in 1822. The result was "A Visit from St. Nicholas." The poem began, "'Twas the night be-fore Christmas," and it presented as St. Nicholas a jolly, globular, sky-riding elf. Moore's St. Nicholas gradually won popularity. Then in 1862, the figure was adopted by Thomas Nast, whose vitriolic pen was the fear of many a candidate for public office. It was Nast who gave Santa his fur-trimmed outfit and who put the finishing touches on the merry old soul we know today *(opposite).*

THOMAS NAST'S SANTA CLAUS *shakes with mirth in a sketch from "Harper's Weekly." This Santa was developed by 1886 and has changed little since.*

CHRISTMAS
AT HOME
ON
THE FARM

The gay family scene at the right is entitled *Christmas at Home*. It came from the brush of a cheerful old lady who began painting when she was 76, and who kept it up, making "a batch" of three or four pictures each week, until she was more than 100 years old. She was Anna Mary Robertson Moses, familiarly known as Grandma Moses, and her bright nostalgic scenes have made her one of the champion Christmas card artists of all time. Nearly 50 million people have received holiday wishes on the back of Grandma's prints.

The secret of her success, Grandma Moses once explained, was that "I like to paint oldtimy things— something real pretty. Most of them are daydreams, as it were." Into *Christmas at Home* she daydreamed a farmhouse parlor much like those in upper New York State and Virginia's Shenandoah Valley, where she spent most of her life. Christmas presents are still being opened and Christmas dinner is being set out on separate tables for the grownups and the children. Almost every detail of the typical farm Christmas is present in the picture—except the two things most closely associated with Christmas in Grandma's mind. One was the scent of hemlock around the Christmas tree, and the other was the smell of varnish on old toys thriftily repainted for a new Christmas.

RECITING "A CHRISTMAS CAROL," *author Dickens (above) stirs an audience to tears.*

DICKENS' CHERISHED CLASSIC

To Charles Dickens, the most popular of Victorian novelists, Christmas was "the only time I know of, in the long calendar of the year when men and women seem by one consent to open their shut-up hearts freely." It was in this spirit that Dickens, in the late fall of 1843, started writing "A Christmas Carol." He finished it in a frenzy, laughing and weeping at his desk. The story of miserly old Scrooge and Tiny Tim and all the others did not catch on immediately. But Dickens popularized it in readings *(above)* before audiences in England and America. The story, part of which appears on pages 92-93, became a 20th Century Christmas classic on film and radio. Some of its characters are illustrated at right and on the next pages by the celebrated English caricaturist Ronald Searle.

CHARACTERS IN THE "CAROL" *include old Scrooge (opposite page), whose chilly meanness "nipped his pointed nose"; a Christmas phantom in black (right, top); and Marley's Ghost (right, bottom), who wore "ghostly spectacles turned up on his ghostly forehead."*

THE GHOST OF CHRISTMAS YET TO COME

THE GHOST OF THE MISERABLE MARLEY

SCROOGE: "A SQUEEZING, WRENCHING, GRASPING, SCRAPING, CLUTCHING, COVETOUS OLD SINNER"

PURSUING A PRETTY LADY, *Scrooge joyfully plays blindman's buff at his nephew's Christmas party. This scene is one of the many visions that*

were shown to the old miser by the Christmas ghosts. Filled with remorse by what he has seen, Scrooge resolves to keep Christmas all year round.

THE CRATCHITS
AT
DINNER

"A Christmas Carol" by Charles Dickens (1812-1870) radiates the mood of benevolence —and sentimentality—that pervaded the Victorian Christmas. This story did as much as any single work to preserve that Victorian mood as a part of today's family Christmas. The happy scene that appears below is taken from a special version prepared by Dickens himself for public readings on his tours of England and America.

Scrooge and the Ghost passed on, invisible, straight to Scrooge's clerk's; and on the threshold of the door the Spirit smiled, and stopped to bless Bob Cratchit's dwelling with the sprinklings of his torch. Think of that! Bob had but fifteen "Bob" a week himself; he pocketed on Saturdays but fifteen copies of his Christian name; and yet the Ghost of Christmas Present blessed his four-roomed house!

Then up rose Mrs. Cratchit, Cratchit's wife, dressed out but poorly in a twice-turned gown, but brave in ribbons, which are cheap and make a goodly show for sixpence; and she laid the cloth, assisted by Belinda Cratchit, second of her daughters, also brave in ribbons; while Master Peter Cratchit plunged a fork into the saucepan of potatoes, and, getting the corners of his monstrous shirt-collar (Bob's private property, conferred upon his son and heir in honor of the day) into his mouth, rejoiced to find himself so gallantly attired, and yearned to show his linen in the fashionable Parks. And now two smaller Cratchits, boy and girl came tearing in, screaming that outside the baker's they had smelt the goose, and known it for their own; and, basking in luxurious thoughts of sage and onion, these young Cratchits danced about the table, and exalted Master Peter Cratchit to the skies, while he (not proud, although his collars nearly choked him) blew the fire, until the slow potatoes, bubbling up, knocked loudly at the saucepan-lid to be let out and peeled.

"What has ever got your precious father then?" said Mrs. Cratchit. "And your brother Tiny Tim! And Martha warn't as late last Christmas day by half an hour!"

"Here's Martha, mother!" said a girl, appearing as she spoke.

"Here's Martha, mother!" cried the two young Cratchits. "Hurrah! There's *such* a goose, Martha!"

"Why, bless your heart alive, my dear, how late you are!" said Mrs. Cratchit, kissing her a dozen times, and taking off her shawl and bonnet for her.

"We'd a deal of work to finish up last night," replied the girl, "and had to clear away this morning, mother!"

"Well! Never mind so long as you are come," said Mrs. Cratchit. "Sit ye down before the fire, my dear, and have a warm, Lord bless ye!"

"No, no! There's father coming," cried the two young Cratchits, who were everywhere at once. "Hide, Martha, hide!"

So Martha hid herself, and in came little Bob, the father, with at least three feet of comforter, exclusive of the fringe, hanging down before him; and his threadbare clothes darned up and brushed, to look seasonable; and Tiny Tim upon his shoulder. Alas for Tiny Tim, he bore a little crutch, and had his limbs supported by an iron frame!

"Why, where's our Martha?" cried Bob Cratchit, looking round.

"Not coming," said Mrs. Cratchit.

"Not coming!" said Bob, with a sudden declension in his high spirits; for he had been Tim's blood-horse all the way from church, and had come home rampant,—"not coming on Christmas day!"

Martha didn't like to see him disappointed, if it were only in joke; so she came out prematurely from behind the closet door, and ran into his arms, while the two young Cratchits hustled Tiny Tim, and bore him off into the wash-house, that he might hear the pudding singing in the copper.

"And how did little Tim behave?" asked Mrs. Cratchit, when she had rallied Bob on his credulity, and Bob had hugged his daughter to his heart's content.

"As good as gold," said Bob, "and better. Somehow he gets thoughtful, sitting by himself so much, and thinks the strangest things you ever heard. He told me, coming home, that he hoped the people saw him in the church, because he was a cripple, and it might be pleasant to them to remember, upon Christmas day, who made lame beggars walk and blind men see."

Bob's voice was tremulous when he told them this, and trembled more when he said that Tiny Tim was growing strong and hearty.

His active little crutch was heard upon the floor, and back came Tiny Tim before another word was spoken, escorted by his brother and sister to his stool beside the fire; and while Bob, turning up his cuffs,—as if, poor fellow, they were capable of being made more shabby,—compounded some hot mixture in a jug with gin and lemons, and stirred it round and round and put it on the hob to simmer, Master Peter and the two ubiquitous young Cratchits went to fetch the goose, with which they soon returned in high procession.

Mrs. Cratchit made the gravy (ready beforehand in a little saucepan) hissing hot; Master Peter mashed the potatoes with incredible vigor; Miss Belinda sweetened up the apple-sauce; Martha dusted the hot plates; Bob took Tiny Tim beside him in a tiny corner at the table; the two young Cratchits set chairs for everybody, not forgetting themselves, and mounting guard upon their posts, crammed spoons into their mouths, lest they should shriek for goose before their turn came to be helped. At last the dishes were set on, and grace was said. It was succeeded by a breathless pause, as Mrs. Cratchit, looking slowly all along the carving-knife, prepared to plunge it in the breast; but when she did,

and when the long-expected gush of stuffing issued forth, one murmur of delight arose all round the board, and even Tiny Tim, excited by the two young Cratchits, beat on the table with the handle of his knife, and feebly cried, Hurrah!

There never was such a goose. Bob said he didn't believe there ever was such a goose cooked. Its tenderness and flavor, size and cheapness, were the themes of universal admiration. Eked out by apple-sauce and mashed potatoes, it was a sufficient dinner for the whole family; indeed, as Mrs. Cratchit said with great delight (surveying one small atom of a bone upon the dish), they hadn't ate it all at last! Yet every one had had enough, and the youngest Cratchits in particular were steeped in sage and onion to the eyebrows! But now, the plates being changed by Miss Belinda, Mrs. Cratchit left the room alone,—too nervous to bear witnesses,—to take the pudding up, and bring it in.

Suppose it should not be done enough! Suppose it should break in turning out! Suppose somebody should have got over the wall of the back yard, and stolen it, while they were merry with the goose,— a supposition at which the two young Cratchits became livid! All sorts of horrors were supposed.

Hallo! A great deal of steam! The pudding was out of the copper. A smell like a washing-day! That was the cloth. A smell like an eating-house and a pastry-cook's next door to each other, with a laundress's next door to that! That was the pudding! In half a minute Mrs. Cratchit entered,— flushed but smiling proudly,—with the pudding, like a speckled cannon-ball, so hard and firm, blazing in half of half a quartern of ignited brandy, and bedight with Christmas holly stuck into the top.

O, a wonderful pudding! Bob Cratchit said, and calmly too, that he regarded it as the greatest success achieved by Mrs. Cratchit since their marriage. Mrs. Cratchit said that now the weight was off her mind she would confess she had had her doubts about the quantity of flour. Everybody had something to say about it, but nobody said or thought it was at all a small pudding for a large family. Any Cratchit would have blushed to hint at such a thing. . . .

There was nothing of high mark in this. They were not a handsome family; they were not well dressed; their shoes were far from being waterproof; their clothes were scanty; and Peter might have known, and very likely did, the inside of a pawnbroker's. But they were happy, grateful, pleased with one another, and contented with the time. . . .

Austrian-born Ludwig Bemelmans (1898-1962) describes the European custom of star-singing in this excerpt from his book "Hansi."

"Christmas Eve," thought Hansi, "should start with the evening. There should be no day on that day at all." Certainly it was the biggest day in the year and the longest to wait around in.

He was sent from the house on errands as soon as he came in. Packages wandered around. One room was locked and even the keyhole stuffed so one could see nothing.

The children weren't hungry though there were the most wonderful things on the table.

"Hansi, nothing is going to happen until this plate is empty. Lieserl, stop wiggling on that chair." Uncle Herman finally looked at his watch and got up. Soon a little silver bell rang, and sparkling across the hall stood the Christmas tree. It turned slowly to music, as glass angels, cookies and burning candles rode around.

The best skis in the whole world are made of Norwegian spruce with long tapered ends. Such a pair stood beside the tree—new and with a binding like that the champion jumpers use. Next to them a skiing cap with a long tassel. Aunt Amalie had knitted it for Hansi. The skis, of course, were from his mother. Uncle Herman had given Hansi a skiing jacket, bright red and warm so that one could get lost and yet stay warm and easily be found in the white snow.

Lieserl had a doll carriage with a big doll dressed like a peasant girl on Sunday. This doll could go to sleep and even said "Mamma," when she was pinched.

"Yes, Lieserl, I see," said Hansi, and looked at his skis again.

Hansi had barely slipped into the skis to try them on and put the stocking cap on his head, when singing was heard outside the house.

"Here they are," said Uncle Herman. Everybody tiptoed to the door, and quietly it swung open.

Three Kings stood majestically in the starry night and sang in verses. They told how they had come from the sands of the desert and were passing this house on the way to visit the Christ Kinderl, to offer Him their precious gifts. Long heavy robes of scarlet flowed off them into the snow. Over their serious devout faces shone tall crowns of pure gold. Their hands were hidden in the deep folds of scarlet sleeves and one of them held a silver lance on which shone the star that had guided the Kings from the East past this house.

After they had finished their song, Uncle Herman invited them to enter his home. He did so singing a verse to which they answered with singing and came in.

Aunt Amalie had brought three cups of hot chocolate and a big plate of Lebkuchen. The Kings seemed to be very hungry indeed after the hard trip from the hot desert and over the cold mountains. Each took three Lebkuchen as they sat down, falling over the plate in their hurry to reach it. One Lebkuchen was left and, as one of the Kings tried to reach for it, the biggest one hit him on the fingers with the silver lance to which was attached the morning star, which broke off and fell into the chocolate. Uncle Herman seemed to know these Kings very well. He took the lances away from them so they would not hurt each other any more.

Lieserl sat down next to the smallest King, who was black, and looked at him very closely. Then she wet her finger and rubbed his nose. The King started to cry and his nose turned white.

"I knew it all the time," said Lieserl. "It's Frau Kofler's little boy Peterl."

Now Hansi came to the table, and he could see that the King, outside of a black face, had only black fingernails. His hands were white—almost white. They were boys from the village. The beautiful stars and crowns were made of cardboard with gold and silver paper pasted over it and the little King was blackened with burnt cork.

They had to sing at three more houses, they said. Aunt Amalie brought two more Lebkuchen, so each could eat another, and Uncle Herman repaired the little King's pale nose with stove blacking. They gave thanks with a little verse for the shelter and food and bowed and walked back into the night. The cold light of the moon gave them back their lost majesty. As they left everyone was serious and quiet. Their stars and crowns had turned again to purest beaten gold.

The evening passed as quickly as the day had been slow in going. Soon it was time to go to midnight services.

This was one of three days in the year when Uncle Herman stood in front of a mirror. He buttoned his tunic and pinned his medals on according to regulation, "six fingers down from the seam of the collar, three fingers over from the second button—right over the heart." Belt and saber were adjusted carefully. Uncle Herman breathed on the buckle and polished it with his sleeve.

Aunt Amalie said, "Why don't you ask for a piece of cloth? It's a shame—the nice new uniform."

The feathers on the green huntsman's hat were straightened out, the white gloves put on.

The children looked up in awe at their new uncle who looked like a picture of his old emperor.

Aunt Amalie had her best dress on with a wide silk shawl around her shoulders and silver lacing from which jingled heavy thalers as she walked. . . .

Aunt Amalie put some things on the table for a small supper when they came back.

The night helped to make Christmas. All the stars were out. The windows of the mountain church shone out into the blue night from the valley and from high up little rows of lights came towards the church. People carried them. They shone up into happy, quiet faces. Silent, holy night—only the bells of the churches rang from near and from the far white fields.

Parisian
Holiday

Paris had a brilliant Christmas in 1876 despite France's recent defeat in the Franco-Prussian War. The holiday is described below in an informal report by Henry James (1843-1916), then New York "Tribune" correspondent in Paris.

. . . But why should I talk of pictures when Paris itself, for the last few days, has formed an immense and brilliant picture. French babies, I believe, hang up their stocking—or put a shoe into the stove—

on New Year's Eve; but Christmas, nevertheless, has been very good-humoredly kept. I have never seen Paris so charming as on this last Christmas Day. The weather put in a claim to a share in the fun, the sky was radiant and the air as soft and pure as a southern spring. It was a day to spend in the streets and all the world did so. I passed it strolling half over the city and wherever I turned I found the entertainment that a pedestrian relishes. What people love Paris for became almost absurdly obvious: charm, beguilement, diversion were stamped upon everything. I confess that, privately, I kept thinking of Prince Bismarck and wishing he might take a turn upon the boulevards. Not that they would have flustered him much, I suppose, for, after all, the boulevards are not human; but the whole spectacle seemed a supreme reminder of the fact so constantly present at this time to the reflective mind —the amazing elasticity of France. Beaten and humiliated on a scale without precedent, despoiled, dishonored, bled to death financially—all this but yesterday—Paris is today in outward aspect as radiant, as prosperous, as instinct with her own peculiar genius as if her sky had never known a cloud. The friendly stranger cannot refuse an admiring glance to this mystery of wealth and thrift and energy and good spirits. I don't know how Berlin looked on Christmas Day, though Christmas-keeping is a German specialty, but I greatly doubt whether its aspect would have appealed so irresistibly to the sympathies of the impartial observer. With the approach of Christmas here the whole line of the boulevards is bordered on each side with a row of little booths for the sale—for the sale of everything conceivable. The width of the classic asphalt is so ample that they form no serious obstruction, and the scene, in the evening especially, presents a picturesque combination of the rustic fair and the highest Parisian civilization. You may buy anything in the line of trifles in the world, from a cotton nightcap to an orange neatly pricked in blue letters with the name of the young lady—Adèle or Ernestine—to whom you may gallantly desire to present it. On the other side of the crowded channel the regular shops present their glittering portals, decorated for the occasion with the latest refinements of the trade. The confectioners in particular are amazing; the rows of marvelous *bonbonnières* look like precious sixteenth-century caskets and reliquaries, chiseled by Florentine artists, in the glass cases of great museums. The *bonbonnière,* in its elaborate and impertinent uselessness, is certainly the consummate flower of material luxury; it seems to bloom, with its petals of satin and its pistils of gold, upon the very apex of the tree of civilization.

A Happy Christmas to You!

OLD-FASHIONED CARDS

Modern Christmas card designs often wander far from traditional themes. In this verse from a poem entitled "Epstein, Spare that Yule Log!" American satirist Ogden Nash rushes to the defense of the time-honored holly and mistletoe.

Oh, give me an old-fashioned Christmas card,
With hostlers hostling in an old inn yard,
With church bells chiming their silver notes,
And jolly red squires in their jolly red coats,
And a good fat goose by the fire that dangles,
And a few more angels and a few less angles.
Turn backward, Time, to please this bard,
And give me an old-fashioned Christmas card.

Sounds of Singing

Bittersweet memories of childhood Christmases in an English country town are evoked here in a stream-of-consciousness poem. Its author is the contemporary English writer Leonard Clark.

*I had almost forgotten the singing in the streets,
Snow piled up by the houses, drifting
Underneath the door into the warm room,*
*Firelight, lamplight, the little lame cat
Dreaming in soft sleep on the hearth, mother dozing,
Waiting for Christmas to come, the boys and me
Trudging over blanket fields waving lanterns to the sky.
I had almost forgotten the smell, the feel of it all,
The coming back home, with girls laughing like stars.
Their cheeks, holly berries, me kissing one,
Silent-tongued, soberly, by the long church wall;
Then back to the kitchen table, supper on the white
    cloth,
Cheese, bread, the home-made wine;
Symbols of the night's joy, a holy feast.
And I wonder now, years gone, mother gone,
The boys and girls scattered, drifted away with the
    snowflakes,
Lamplight done, firelight over,
If the sounds of our singing in the streets are still there,
Those old tunes, still praising;
And now, a life-time of Decembers away from it all,
A branch of remembering holly spears my cheeks,
And I think it may be so;
Yes, I believe it may be so.*

CHURCHILL'S CHRISTMAS IN THE WHITE HOUSE

Thoughts of children at Christmas inspired the speech which Winston Churchill made to the American people during a wartime visit in 1941.

I spend this anniversary and festival far from my country, far from my family, and yet I cannot truthfully say that I feel far from home. Whether it be the ties of blood on my mother's side, or the friendships I have developed here over many years of active life, or the commanding sentiment of comradeship in the common cause of great peoples who speak the same language, who kneel at the same altars and, to a very large extent, pursue the same ideals; I cannot feel myself a stranger here in the centre and at the summit of the United States. I feel a sense of unity and fraternal association which, added to the kindliness of your welcome, convinces me that I have a right to sit at your fireside and share your Christmas joys.

Fellow workers, fellow soldiers in the cause, this

is a strange Christmas Eve. Almost the whole world is locked in deadly struggle. Armed with the most terrible weapons which science can devise, the nations advance upon each other. Ill would it be for us this Christmastide if we were not sure that no greed for the lands or wealth of any other people, no vulgar ambitions, no morbid lust for material gain at the expense of others, had led us to the field. Ill would it be for us if that were so. Here, in the midst of war, raging and roaring over all the lands and seas, sweeping nearer to our hearths and homes; here, amid all these tumults, we have tonight the peace of the spirit in each cottage home and in every generous heart. Therefore we may cast aside, for this night at least, the cares and dangers which

beset us and make for the children an evening of happiness in a world of storm. Here then, for one night only, each home throughout the English-speaking world should be a brightly-lighted island of happiness and peace.

Let the children have their night of fun and laughter, let the gifts of Father Christmas delight their play. Let us grown-ups share to the full in their unstinted pleasures before we turn again to the stern tasks and the formidable years that lie before us, resolved that by our sacrifice and daring these same children shall not be robbed of their inheritance or denied their right to live in a free and decent world.

And so, in God's mercy, a happy Christmas to you all.

God Rest You Merry

One of the most popular of Christmas carols, especially in England, is reproduced below. Over the years it has been sung to at least two tunes. This familiar melody was printed and offered for sale in London as early as the 1790s.

VII

A LIVING TRADITION

THE NATURAL TENDENCY OF time to obliterate ancient customs, and silence ancient sports, is too much promoted by the utilitarian spirit of the day; and they who would have no man enjoy, without being able to give a reason for the enjoyment which is in him, are robbing life of half its beauty, and some of its virtues. If the old festivals and hearty commemorations....had no other recommendations than their *convivial* character —the community of enjoyment which they imply—they would, on that account alone, be worthy of all promotion....We love all which tends to call man from the solitary and chilling pursuit of his own separate and selfish views, into the warmth of common sympathy, and within the bands of a common brotherhood.

"THE BOOK OF CHRISTMAS," THOMAS K. HERVEY

THE MUMMERS PARADE *in Philadelphia features elaborate costumes, as did medieval celebrations during the Christmas season.*

A PROFUSION
OF FEASTS
AND CUSTOMS

GLOWING CANDLES *illuminate the interior of Old Swede's Church, Philadelphia, during the celebration of the Lucia light festival.*

CHRISTMAS TODAY in the United States is celebrated with a multitude of traditions—some ancient, some comparatively recent; some devout, some secular; some transplanted from European homelands; a few—among Indians and Eskimos—partly indigenous.

A public observance for all the nation is the lighting of the tree on the White House lawn by the President—a custom originated by Warren G. Harding. But there is hardly an American town that does not have some Christmas observance of its own in which local citizens may actively participate. On Boston's Beacon Hill, strolling carolers converge on Louisburg Square, whose householders put candles in the windows to light the songsters' way. In Seattle, foreign communities, consulates and church groups join in presenting a festival which depicts "Christmas around the World" staged with authentic foreign costumes, music and refreshments.

"Christmas Trees around the World" is a favorite theme of similar festivals. In Dallas, for example, a dozen trees are displayed, each one placed before a backdrop representing a custom or legend of a different country. In Atlanta the Christmas trees share a display with crèches of various nations—an Italian crèche of glass, a French Provençal crèche with carved wood figures, brilliantly decorated in paint.

Countless plays and pageants are presented. A Lutheran church in North Hollywood builds a 200-foot-long stage-set of Bethlehem; four parishioners dressed as Roman heralds on horseback announce Caesar's decree, while others in appropriate costumes play the parts of angels and shepherds. In church vestries and parish houses in every state, mothers straighten the robes of many small Wise Men, and paper-winged angels rehearse their lines.

Some events of the Christmas season have been deliberately started in emulation of old customs. Palmer Lake, Colorado, holds a Yule log hunt on the Sunday before Christmas. A four-foot log is hidden in the mountains outside town, and the finder drags it back to City Hall, where it is set afire. The Philadelphia Mummers Parade, held on New Year's Day, echoes a tradition of masked revelry that dates back to the Roman *kalends,* and that was practiced with highly elaborate costumes and wild pantomime in medieval and Renaissance festivities at Christmastime.

Many Americans still observe the customs of their ancestors from foreign lands. Polish Catholic families on Christmas Eve break and share the thin wafer called *oplatek,* a symbol of love and devotion. Moravian communities in Winston-Salem, North Carolina, and Bethlehem, Pennsylvania, continue the custom of *putz-ing*—making tiny figures to decorate the tree—and of distributing beeswax candles at Christmas Eve services as a reminder that Christ came to be the Light of the World.

Light is the theme, too, of the Swedish Lucia Fest—the festival of St. Lucy. Eight boys carrying golden stars lead a procession into the church; then youngsters dressed as elves skip down the aisle to a pot of food left for them *(opposite).* They are followed by 30 girls in white, carrying candles. At the end comes a lovely girl dressed as Lucia, crowned with seven burning candles. And everyone sings old Swedish carols.

In Alaska, Eskimos celebrate Christmas with the feasts (reindeer roast and a dessert of foamy seal blubber with blueberries) and the games (weight lifting, broad jumping and the like) which their ancestors held in pre-Christian times to mark the winter solstice. In the Southwest, Indians have blended their ancient legends of the battle between good and evil with the Christmas story as it was taught them by Spanish missionaries. The drama that results is frequently danced out with steps from the Indians' rain and fertility rites.

Thus millions of Americans, each in his own way, observe Christmas with countless combinations of colorful customs and traditions. In many instances the celebrations are 20th Century echoes of rites practiced hundreds—and even thousands—of years ago; others are clearly modern inventions inserted into the complex texture of Christmas rejoicing. But for all who celebrate in whatever fashion, Christmas remains an occasion to enjoy friends and family, a day full of the love and generosity that the first Christmas of all inspired in man's heart.

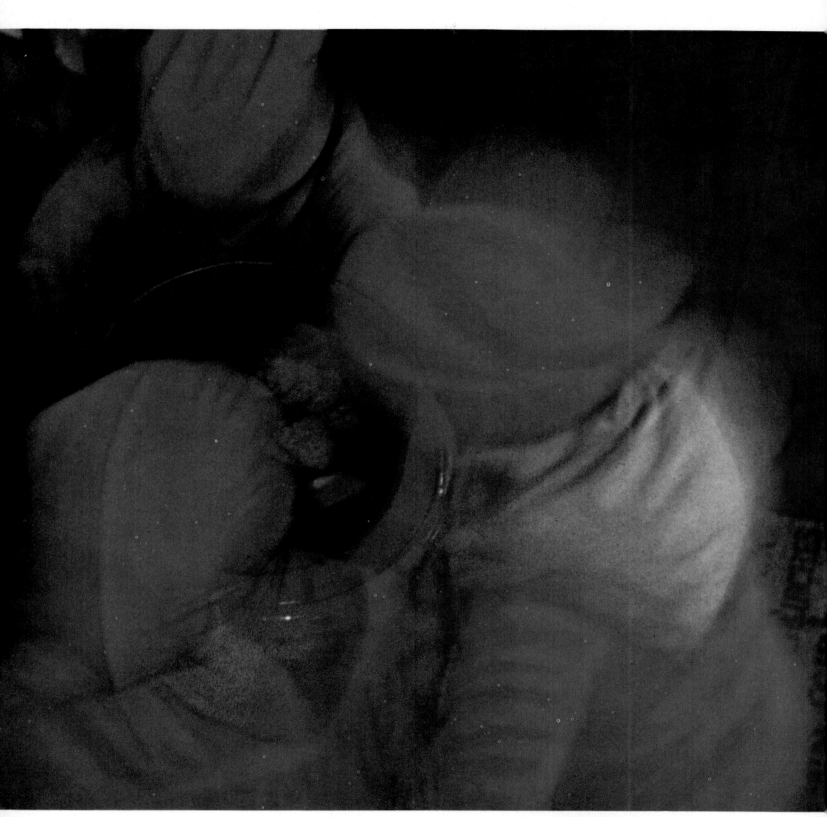

CHRISTMAS ELVES *costumed in scarlet gather around the pot of food left for them at the Lucia Fest in the Old Swede's Church in Philadelphia. The festival of St. Lucy, whose name suggests light ("lux") and whose feast day (December 13) falls close to the winter solstice when the days begin to lengthen, is a Swedish tradition widely observed in Swedish-American communities.*

ROCHESTER'S BONFIRE *lights up Twelfth Night in upstate New York. Discarded Christmas trees are piled 25 feet high and set aflame on the Lake Ontario shore. Girl Scouts sing carols and Boy Scouts throw snowballs as the holiday season ends with this gargantuan blaze.*

HOLIDAY
FIRES
AND FIREWORKS

Similarities in holiday customs often suggest connections that never existed or that have long since been lost. For example, the Chinese have for centuries celebrated their New Year with fireworks to dispel evil spirits. But in parts of the American South, where firecrackers were long used on Christmas, their only purpose was to produce a loud noise. And Williamsburg, Virginia, where Christmas is observed in the colonial manner, fires its 18th Century cannon *(opposite)* simply as a parting salute to the holiday.

Similarly, many pagans of olden times and northern lands burned midwinter bonfires to speed the returning sun. Medieval Christians also burned winter bonfires, but as a practical way of disposing of holiday greenery. For the same reason —and for the fun of it, too—Christmas trees are burned today *(above)*.

WILLIAMSBURG'S GUNFIRE *marks the day after Christmas in Virginia. In the previous week, the old colonial city holds a "grand illumination," with every window candlelit.*

AT MIDNIGHT MASS *in a candlelit cave at Bethlehem, South Dakota, Catholic communicants greet the arrival of Christmas. The natural cavern, known as the Shrine of the Nativity, is reminiscent of the cave beneath the Church of the Nativity in the Holy Land's Bethlehem. The Christmas Mass is being celebrated by the prior of a Black Hills Benedictine mission on the site.*

WORSHIP,
THE HEART
OF THE HOLIDAY

In its basic character, Christmas remains deeply religious in spite of the secular festivities that have grown up around it. Christians never forget that the day commemorates the miraculous birth of a baby in whom God was incarnate. The Gospel according to St. Luke strongly suggests that Jesus was born at night. And so there arose in the Western Church, as early as 400 A.D., the custom of holding midnight Mass on Christmas Eve *(opposite)*. Earlier still, Epiphany, January 6, had been celebrated in the Eastern Orthodox Church. "Epiphany," a Greek word meaning "showing forth," refers to the three manifestations of Christ's divinity which traditionally occurred on that date: the Adoration of the Magi, His baptism by St. John, and His first miracle, the changing of water into wine at the marriage feast at Cana. To this day Epiphany remains more important to the Orthodox Churches than to others, and they celebrate it with a number of ceremonies involving water *(below)*. The third great division of Christianity, the Protestant sects, also celebrates Christ's birthday with widely divergent customs and reverent services.

IN THE LUCIA FEST, *a youthful procession in Philadelphia's Old Swede's Church is followed by a girl with a crown of candles representing Lucia (St. Lucy). This celebration of lights has been held here for 25 years.*

ON EPIPHANY, *the Greek Orthodox community of Tarpon Springs, Florida, celebrates an ancient ceremony at the water's edge. The bishop (above) blesses the waters, then throws in a cross. Young men of the congregation dive after the cross, and the one who retrieves it (right) is specially blessed.*

105

CUSTOMS ECHOING THE DISTANT PAST

The wedding of Christian and pagan traditions at Christmas is uniquely exemplified by the Boar's Head and Yule Log ceremony of the Trinity Episcopal Cathedral in Cleveland, Ohio, pictured on these pages. The yule log tradition, believed to have come from Scandinavia, survives as proof of early Christianity's tolerance of pagan ritual. From pre-Christian times the burning of a log at the end of the year appears to have represented banishment of the old year's evil and a rekindling of the hearth fire, the center of family life. Its ashes were often scattered to bring good luck far and wide, and a part of the log was saved to light the next season's fire. The boar's head (which for the sake of convenience is sometimes represented by a suckling pig or even a pork roast) is thought by some authorities to have been eaten originally in honor of Frey, a Scandinavian deity whose symbol was the boar.

The particular ritual practiced in Cleveland has been traced back well over 100 years. It was brought to colonial America by a French Huguenot family named Bouton, who picked it up on their way through England and passed it on to a descendant. Established at the Hoosick School in Hoosick, New York, in 1888, the custom was later transplanted to Christ Church, Cincinnati, and thence to Cleveland.

The ceremony commences when a trumpeter *(opposite)* sounds three clarion calls. Costumed trenchermen carry in the boar's head on a large litter. Following them comes a group of scarlet-costumed bearers *(left)* called "sprites," who bring in the yule log. Then a soloist sings: "The boar's head in hand bear I, bedecked with bays and rosemary; and I pray you, my masters, be merry, as many as are at this feast." And the congregation responds in Latin with the following chorus: "The boar's head I bring, giving praises to God."

YULE LOG SPRITES *bring in their contribution to the Christmas ceremony at Trinity Episcopal Cathedral, Cleveland. The practice, introduced in 1959, recalls customs established in the mists of antiquity.*

THE BOAR'S HEAD TRUMPETER, *standing before a stained-glass window of Cleveland's cathedral, signals the start of a Christmas procession that suggests customs of medieval England.*

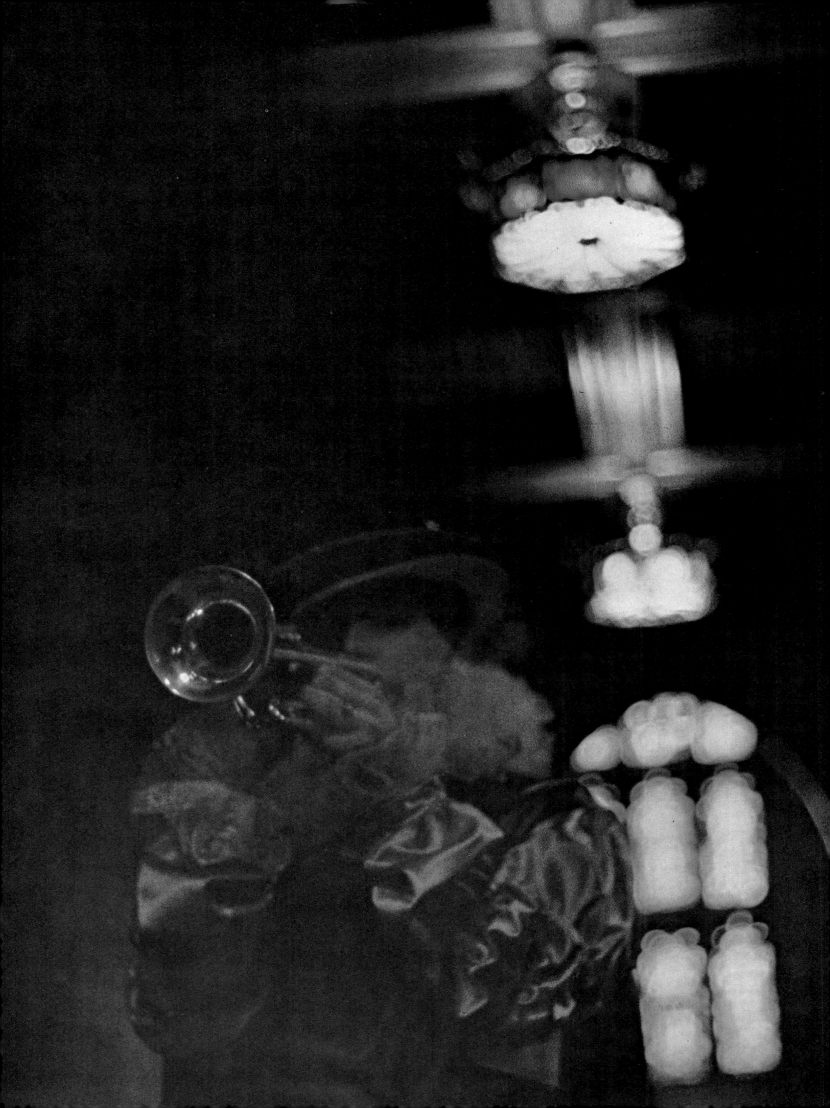

IN THIS VOLUME
ANTHOLOGY SELECTIONS

CHRISTMAS MUSIC

INDEX

* This symbol preceding a page number indicates a photograph or painting of the subject mentioned

PICTURE CREDITS

Illustrations on each page are listed from left to right and from top to bottom. In the case of paintings and works of sculpture, the artist's name, if known, is given in capitals—e.g., FRA ANGELICO; the name of the photographer or the picture agency appears in parentheses—e.g., (Eric Schaal).

mette). 23—Month of December from a late-14th Century calendar, MS Rawl. D.939, Courtesy Bodleian Library, Oxford. 24, 25—Capture of Jerusalem and Crowning of King of Jerusalem, two 14th Century miniatures from *Chronique d'Outremer* by GODEFROI DE BUILLON, MS Français 352, Courtesy Bibliothèque Nationale, Paris. 27—Woodcuts by Fritz Kredel. 28—January, 15th Century miniature from *Très Riches Heures du Duc de Berry*, Courtesy Musée Condé, Chantilly (Fernand Bourges). 30—Le Gâteau de Rois, detail of 15th Century miniature from *Heures d'Adélaïde de Savoie*, Courtesy Musée Condé, Chantilly (Photo Giraudon). 31—Boar Hunt, 15th Century French miniature, Courtesy The Wildenstein Foundation, Inc. (Frank Lerner for TIME). 32—*Le Roi Charles VII en Mage*, 15th Century miniature from *Heures d'Etienne Chevalier* by JEAN FOUQUET, MS 187, Courtesy Musée Condé, Chantilly (Photo Giraudon)—Mummers, marginal decoration from 14th Century Flemish manuscript, *Romance of Alexander the Great*, MS Bodley 264, Courtesy Bodleian Library, Oxford. 33—St. George and the Dragon, 15th Century miniature from *The Belles Heures of Jean, Duke of Berry*, Courtesy The Metropolitan Museum of Art, The Cloisters Collection, New York, Purchase, 1954 (Robert Crandall). 34, 35—Tournament, 15th Century miniature from *Chronique du Hainaut* by JACQUES DE GUISSE, Courtesy Bibliothèque Royale, Brussels (Frank Scherschel), King John, 14th Century miniature from *Chronicle of Peter Langtoft*, MS Royal 20 A II, Courtesy The British Museum, London (Larry Burrows)—Jousting, 15th Century miniature from *The Luttrel Psalter*, Courtesy the British Museum, London (Frank Scherschel). 36—St. Francis preaching to the birds, 14th Century stained glass window from Königsfelden, Switzerland, Courtesy Iris Verlag, Laupen near Bern. 37—Miracle Play, Plate 22 from Volume Nine of Josef Gregor's *Monumenta Scenica*, published in Vienna by the Management of the National Library with the support of the Society for the Publication of Monuments of the Theatre (Eric Schaal). 38—*Christkindwiege*, 15th Century rocking cradle from South Germany, Courtesy Bayerisches Nationalmuseum, Munich. 39—Meister Heinrich Frauenlob's Music School, 14th Century miniature from the Manessa Codex, MS 848, Courtesy Heidelberg University Library. 41—Woodcuts by Fritz Kredel. 42—German Christmas tree, 16th Century colored parchment, Courtesy Germanisches Nationalmuseum, Nuremberg. 44, 45—Henry VIII and his jester Will Somers, from a Psalter written for Henry VIII by IOHANNES MALLARD, Courtesy The British Museum, London, Queen Elizabeth and the Earl of Leicester dancing, 16th Century oil painting by an unknown artist, by kind permission of Viscount De L'Isle V.C., G.C.M.G., G.C.V.O. from his Penshurst Place Collection (Derek Bayes). 46, 47—INIGO JONES's pen and ink wash sketches for *Oberon* and colored sketch for *Hymen*, Devonshire Collection, Chatsworth. Reproduced by permission of the Trustees of the Chatsworth Settlement (Derek Bayes). 48—*Twelfth Night Feast*, 17th Century oil painting by JAN STEEN, Courtesy Museum of Fine Arts, Boston. 49—*The Feast of St. Nicholas*, 17th Century oil painting by JAN STEEN, Courtesy Rijksmuseum, Amsterdam. 50—Contemporary cast from 17th Century German cake mold, Courtesy Germanisches Nationalmuseum, Nuremberg. 51—Early 17th Century Norwegian wall hanging from Lome in the County of Christian, Courtesy Nordic Museum, Stockholm. 55—Indian, watercolor by FERDINAND BADIN, Courtesy Buffalo Historical Society, Buffalo. 57—Woodcuts by Fritz Kredel. 58—*Assembly at Wanstead House*, 18th Century oil painting, WILLIAM HOGARTH, Courtesy Philadelphia Museum of Art, Philadelphia, John Howard McFadden Collection (Fernand Bourges). 60, 61—18th Century marionettes owned by the Grimani Family at Cà Rezzonico, Venice (David Lees). 62, 63—*Knecht Ruprecht*, copper engraving by FRANZ REGIS GOZ, 1784, *Twelfth Night Waits*, 18th Century oil painting by CORNELIS TROOST, Courtesy Royal Cabinet of Paintings, The Hague. 64—18th Century Nuremberg Christmas Market, Courtesy Germanisches Nationalmuseum, Nuremberg. 65—Drawing of Moravian Love Feast Service, dated 1757, Courtesy Old Salem, Inc. 66—*High Life Below Stairs*, by ROBERT CRUIKSHANK, Courtesy The Mansell Collection, London. 71—Woodcuts by Fritz Kredel. 72—Victorian Christmas card, Courtesy Victoria and Albert Museum, London (Derek Bayes). 74—*The Christmas Wine*, by RALPH CALDICOTT, Courtesy The Mansell Collection, London (Derek Bayes). 75—*Christmas Plum Pudding*, by SEYMOUR, Courtesy The Mansell Collection, London (Derek Bayes). 76, 77—*The Half Hour before Dinner*, unknown artist, *The Christmas Dinner*, by SEYMOUR—*Christmas*, by GEORGE CRUIK-SHANK, Courtesy The Mansell Collection, London (Derek Bayes). 78—*Weinacht ist da*, German print c. 1850 (Historia Photo). 79—*Bénédiction de la Bûche en Alsace*, Courtesy Editions B. Arthaud, Grenoble—*Lucia*, pen and ink drawing by FRITZ VAN DARDEL, Courtesy Nordic Museum, Stockholm. 80, 81—Christmas celebration in Russia c. 1860 (The Bettmann Archive), Serbian Christmas cake, 1875 (Culver Pictures)—*Christmas Oracle in Swabia*, 19th Century drawing by LOUIS BRAUN (Historisches Bildarchiv). 82, 83—Culver Pictures. 84—Illustrations from "A Visit to St. Nicholas" from *The Evergreen*, December 1849, Courtesy The New York Historical Society, New York. 85—"Santa Claus," THOMAS NAST's drawing for *Harper's Weekly*, c. 1865, Courtesy The New York Historical Society, New York. 86, 87—*Christmas at Home* by GRANDMA MOSES, (c) Grandma Moses Properties, Inc., Courtesy Galerie St. Etienne, New York. 88 through 92—*Charles Dickens' Last Reading* (Radio Times Hulton Picture Library), Illustrations from "A Christmas Carol" by RONALD SEARLE, Copyright (c) 1960 by Ronald Searle. By permission of the World Library. 96—Sy Seidman. 97—Woodcuts by Fritz Kredel. 98—Robert Phillips. 100—Fred Ward from Black Star. 101—Michel Lambeth. 102, 103—Michel Lambeth, Robert Phillips. 104—A. Y. Owen. 105—Fred Ward from Black Star—Flip Schulke from Black Star. 106, 107—Michel Lambeth.

FOR FURTHER READING

Barnett, James H., *The American Christmas*. Macmillan, 1954.

Carpenter, Edward, *Pagan and Christian Creeds; Their Origin and Meaning*. London, George Allen & Unwin, 1921.

Chambers, E. K., *The Medieval Stage*. Oxford University Press, 1903.

Chute, Marchette, *Ben Jonson of Westminster*. E. P. Dutton & Co., 1953.

Count, Earl W., *4,000 Years of Christmas*. Henry Schuman, 1948.

Crippen, T. C., *Christmas and Christmas Lore*. London, Blackie & Son, N. D.

Cullmann, Oscar, *The Early Church*. Westminster Press, 1956.

Dawson, W. F., *Christmas: Its Origins and Associations*. London, Elliot Stock, 1902.

Evans, Joan, *Art in Mediaeval France, 987-1498*. Oxford University Press, 1948.

Foley, Daniel J., *Christmas in the Good Old Days*. Chilton Company, 1961.

Frazer, Sir James George, *The Golden Bough*. Macmillan, 1923.

Fremantle, Anne, *A Treasury of Early Christianity*. Mentor Books, 1960.

Frost, Lesley, *Come Christmas*. Coward-McCann, 1929.

Greene, Richard L., *A Selection of English Carols*. Oxford University Press, 1962.

Hadfield, Miles and John, *The Twelve Days of Christmas*. Little, Brown & Co., 1962.

Harrison, Michael, *The Story of Christmas*. London, Odhams Press, N. D.

Hervey, Thomas K., *The Book of Christmas*. London, William Spooner, 1836.

Hole, Christina, *Christmas and its Customs*. M. Barrows & Co., 1958.

Hottes, Alfred Carl, *1001 Christmas Facts and Fancies*. A. T. de la Mare Company, 1954.

Huizinga, J., *The Waning of the Middle Ages*. London, Arnold, 1924.

Hutchinson, Paul & Winfred E. Garrison, *20 Centuries of Christianity*. Harcourt, Brace and Co., 1959.

Irving, Washington, *The Sketch Book*. Dodd Mead, 1954.

Jacobus de Voragine, *The Golden Legend*. Longmans, Green & Co., 1948.

FOR FURTHER READING *continued*

Kane, Harnett T., *The Southern Christmas Book*. Rand McKay, 1958.

Krythe, Mamie R., *All About Christmas*. Harper & Bros., 1954.

Lewis, D. B. Wyndham & G. C. Heseltine, *A Christmas Book, an Anthology for Moderns*. E. P. Dutton & Co., 1951.

Miles, Clement A., *Christmas in Ritual and Tradition*. London, T. Fisher Unwin, 1912.

Runciman, Steven, *A History of the Crusades*. Cambridge University Press, 1951.

Sandys, William, *Christmastide, its History, Festivities and Carols*. London, John Russell Smith, N. D.

Sechrist, Elizabeth Hough, and Janette Woolsey, *It's Time for Christmas*. Macrae Smith Company, 1959.

Shoemaker, Alfred L., *Christmas in Pennsylvania*. Pennsylvania Folklife Society, 1959.

Spicer, Dorothy, *Festivals of Western Europe*. H. W. Wilson Co., 1958.

Swedish Christmas. Compiled and issued by Ewert Cagner in cooperation with Goran Axel-Nilsson and Henrik Sandblad, Tre Tryckare, Gothenburg, 1955.

Vloberg, Maurice, *Les Noels de France*. Paris, B. Arthaud, 1953.

Weiser, Francis X., *The Christmas Book*. Harcourt Brace, 1952.

Wernecke, Herbert H., *Christmas Customs Around the World*. Westminster Press, 1959.

Wernecke, Herbert H., *Celebrating Christmas Around the World*. Westminster Press, 1962.

ACKNOWLEDGMENTS

The editors of this volume are particularly indebted to Professor Earl W. Count, Chairman of the Department of Anthropology, Hamilton College, who read and commented on the complete text; to Monsignor Myles M. Bourke, Professor of New Testament, St. Joseph's Seminary, Dunwoodie, Yonkers, New York, and Professor W. D. Davies, Edward Robinson Professor of Biblical Theology, Union Theological Seminary, New York; to Byron Dobell, who initiated the project and saw it through its earliest stages, and to Daniel Longwell, former Chairman of the Board of Editors of LIFE. The editors are also grateful to the Reverend Lowrie John Daly, S.J., of St. Louis University, Brother William J. Kiefer, S.M., John Hadfield, J.A.R. Pimlott, Randolph E. Haugan, Margaret Reynolds and Bernice E. Leary, all of whom generously made available the results of their extensive research into the history of Christmas; to Frederick B. Adams Jr., Director, Pierpont Morgan Library; the Library of Congress Prints and Photographs Division; the New York Public Library; Bettmann Archive, Inc.; Culver Pictures, Inc.; the New York Historical Society; the Howard University Library; the Frick Art Reference Library; the Walters Art Gallery, Baltimore; The Metropolitan Museum of Art, New York; the Victoria and Albert Museum, London; the numerous European museums, libraries and art galleries cited in the credits on pages 110-111; and the many other individuals who contributed valuable assistance.

Grateful acknowledgment is made for permission to reprint, in whole or in part, the following selections:

P. 9 From *The Ecclesiastical History of the English Nation, and Other Writings*, by The Venerable Bede. Texts by J. Stevens and John Stevenson. Everyman's Library. Reprinted by permission of E. P. Dutton & Co., Inc., New York, and J. M. Dent & Sons, Ltd., London.

P. 16 From *Times Three* by Phyllis McGinley, copyright (C) 1958 by Phyllis McGinley. Reprinted by permission of The Viking Press, Inc., New York, and Martin Secker and Warburg, Ltd., London.

Pp. 26-27 From *A Christmas Book: An Anthology for Moderns*, compiled by D. B. Wyndham Lewis and G. C. Heseltine. Published by E. P. Dutton & Co., Inc., New York, and J. M. Dent & Sons, Ltd., London, and reprinted with their permission.

P. 29 From *The Yorkist Age* by Paul Murray Kendall. Copyright (C) 1962 by Paul Murray Kendall. Reprinted by permission of W. W. Norton & Company, Inc., New York, and George Allen & Unwin, Ltd., London.

P. 40 *The Journal of Christopher Columbus*, translated by Cecil Jane. Copyright 1960 by Clarkson N. Potter, Inc., New York. Reprinted by permission of Clarkson N. Potter, Inc., and Anthony Blond Ltd., London.

Pp. 40-41 *The Shorter Cambridge Medieval History*, by C. W. Previté-Orton Volume II. Published by the Syndics of the Cambridge University Press, New York and London, 1952.

Pp. 52-53 *Shakespeare's Christmas Gift to Queen Bess in the Year 1596*, by Anna Bennefon McMahan. Published by A. C. McClurg & Co., Chicago, 1907. Reprinted with permission.

Pp. 54-55 *The Gentleman of Renaissance France*, by W. L. Wiley. Published by Harvard University Press, Cambridge, copyright 1954.

P. 57 English translation of lyrics for "Twas in the Moon of Wintertime" (Huron Indian Carol) used by permission of the Copyright Owner, The Frederick Harris Music Co. Ltd., Oakville, Ontario.

P. 68 *Christmas with the Washingtons*, by Olive Bailey, drawings by Worth Bailey, published by The Dietz Press, Inc., Richmond, 1948. Reprinted with permission.

Pp. 94-95 From *Hansi* by Ludwig Bemelmans. Copyright (C) 1934, 1962 by Ludwig Bemelmans. Reprinted by permission of The Viking Press, Inc., New York.

P. 96 From *Verses from 1929 On* by Ogden Nash. Copyright 1933 by Ogden Nash. Reprinted by permission of Little, Brown & Company, Boston, and J. M. Dent & Sons, Ltd., London.

Production Staff for Time Incorporated
Arthur J. Murphy Jr. (Vice President and Director of Production)
Robert E. Foy, James P. Menton and Caroline Ferri
Body text photocomposed under the direction of
Albert J. Dunn and Arthur J. Dunn

X